'This book is of enormous value to ev̶ not just the makers of films. Essentially, it describes how to create and deliver a vital message with the greatest likelihood of bringing about change. It is encyclopaedic – from every practical aspect of film-making to various inspirational case studies to a well-chosen list of further reading. The introduction by the authors is current, heartfelt and motivating for today's conservation film-makers – your work *must* make a difference!'
– Lee Durrell MBE, PhD, Honorary Director, Durrell Wildlife Conservation Trust

'This terrific book will become the bible for everyone determined to fly in the face of everything-is-wonderful-and-happy natural history programmes and show, instead, that conservation can be awe-inspiring and watchable, too.'
– Mark Carwardine, Conservationist

'Veteran film-makers Madelaine Westwood and Piers Warren have written a fascinating book focused on the nexus of film-making and conservation. Beginning with an introduction full of passionate eloquence, the book is at once an inspiring denunciation of the films made by the networks, a practical and invaluable guide to how to make powerful and effective conservation films, and a plea to make environmental films ethically. *Conservation Film-making* is a richly nourishing book, a professional *tour de force*, and a compelling argument that films, when made according to the best practices contained in this book, can make a huge and positive difference to the world in which we live. I wish a book like this had existed when I first got into wildlife film-making three decades ago. Please do your career a favour and read Westwood and Warren's guidance and advice.'
– Professor Chris Palmer, author of *Shooting in the Wild* and *Confessions of a Wildlife Filmmaker*, Distinguished Film Producer in Residence at American University, and Director of the Center for Environmental Filmmaking in Washington, DC.

'"Conservation is boring!" "Conservation is the story of heroic actions by courageous people to save a species/protect the environment/save the world." Judging by the lack of conservation films on the main TV channels, most TV executives agree with the first statement. Perhaps this outstanding guide on 'How to make films that make a difference' will change their view to the second, more accurate statement. *Conservation Film-making* is a detailed and well-researched 'how to' guide, but it is more than that – it's a good read! The book is most compelling when, like the films it espouses, it tells stories: filming trips that went wrong; successful campaign films; viral videos – 'mind bombs' – that changed the world. If we are to prevent dangerous climate change and halt biodiversity loss, we need to engage every person on the planet. Film is the most powerful tool in the conservationist's toolbox, and this book will help us make better films, target them for the right audience and monitor the results. It should be read by everyone involved in conservation, to understand better how film could – indeed should – be used.'

– Ian Redmond OBE, Chairman of Ape Alliance, Ambassador for the UNEP Convention on Migratory Species

CONSERVATION FILM-MAKING

How to make films that make a difference

MADELAINE WESTWOOD AND PIERS WARREN

FOREWORD BY JANE GOODALL

Published by:

Wildeye
United Kingdom

Email: info@wildeye.co.uk
Website: www.wildeye.co.uk/publishing

ISBN 978-1-905843-10-7

Many thanks to;
Roland Clare for copy-editing (www.wordfix.org)
Chantal Palmer for cover design
David Badger for images
Jason Peters, Simon Beer, Laura Turner, Lee Thompson, Peter Toll, Mihali Moore, Dee Marshall, Chris Palmer, Archie Ruff and John Metcalfe for support and advice

And to those who helped out with the case studies:
Mike Pandey, Maarten van Rouveroy, Julian Newman, Sandy Watt, Shekar Dattatri, Nigel Butcher, Rob Stewart, Will Anderson, Ben Please, Neil Grubb, Rob Spray and Abbie Barnes

Contents

Various resources and web links are referred to throughout this book, but that is just a starting point. For more comprehensive resources, we recommend exploring the directories at www.wildlife-film.com, where you can find, listed and described, many production companies, film festivals, broadcasters, footage libraries, distributors, film-making freelancers and more.

Foreword

For all of us who care about the environment and wildlife – and want to make a difference – this is an important book.

Very early in my career I discovered how powerful documentary films can be. When I arrived at Cambridge University to work on a PhD, I was shocked to be told, by some of the professors, that I could not write about chimpanzees' personalities, problem-solving abilities nor, above all, emotions. All those attributes were unique to humans, I was told. Of course, having grown up with a dog, I knew the professors were wrong – but these things are hard to prove. Then *National Geographic* sent Hugo van Lawick to make a documentary film. And it was when his early footage of the Gombe chimpanzees was shown on TV that even some of the most critical scientists realised I had not been anthropomorphising, but simply reporting fact. Images of Flo's child, Flint, huddled and grieving after losing his mother, went straight to people's hearts. Shots of chimpanzees using and making tools to 'fish' for termites proved what my words alone could not.

A short while ago in Hong Kong I had the opportunity to watch a class of children reacting to a film about ivory poaching. They all knew about this ecological crisis – they had had a verbal account – but now they were watching images: a baby elephant playing in the water, splashing with his trunk; another suckling while his mother gently stroked him with her trunk. Then suddenly a park ranger was approaching a dead elephant, her face bloody where her tusks had been hacked out, her trunk cut off and lying nearby. And finally film of an orphaned baby elephant, deeply depressed, listless and grieving. Then – and only then – did the children truly understand exactly what the ivory trade meant for the elephants. Film is so much more powerful than words alone.

It is clear that documentary films can change attitudes, and can thus be powerful tools in our fight to save vanishing wildlife. But they need to be good films, or people will switch off. Having worked closely with many film-makers – I was married to one of them! – I learned some of the skills that are most valuable for making a good film. You need to know just what aspects of the situation, or subject, must be focused upon, but also to be ready to take advantage of

7

something new and unexpected if it happens in front of your lens. And, if you are filming animals, you need to be patient and sufficiently attuned to the subjects to be able to predict what they will do, when and where. A film must capture the attention of the targeted audience, must move quickly, must show aspects of nature, or aspects of an issue, that may be new, or be filmed in a new way. And this can often be accomplished by skilled editing.

Another important aspect of making a good film is the commentary. Some good documentaries are ruined by too much talking, or by the wrong kind of voice. And it is important, too, to combine the visuals with just the right music. Not the sort that is churned out on so many YouTube clips, which I always have to put on mute! Music that actually complements and adds to the visual image can make the message even more powerful. In fact there are some documentaries in which images and music are so brilliantly combined that there is no need for spoken commentary. This means there will be no need for translation – the film will speak to the global community and inspire it to take action.

Madelaine Westwood has years of experience in making top-quality wildlife and conservation documentaries, and she and Piers Warren have been training people to make films themselves for well over a decade. But not everyone can attend their workshops, which is why they have written *Conservation Film-making*. It explains all the aspects of this complex subject that you need to know to make your own documentaries. And it emphasises, also, that you do not need the latest and most expensive gear to make a good film. You need passion, commitment and a deep understanding of your subject. Then you will be able to use film to explain your cause, and play your part in changing attitudes towards the natural world, before it is too late. I look forward to sharing this knowledge with our 'Roots & Shoots' global network, the Jane Goodall Institute's humanitarian and environmental movement for young people in over 130 countries.

Madelaine and Piers, thank you for writing it.

Jane Goodall PhD, DBE
Founder of the Jane Goodall Institute, and UN Messenger of Peace
www.janegoodall.org

Introduction

Conservation: the action of conserving something; the preservation, protection, or restoration of the natural environment and of wildlife [OED]

The journal *Current Biology* recently published an article – *The Importance and Benefits of Species* – that advocated a conservation philosophy that all species are important, regardless of their usefulness to humans, apparent value, intelligence or attractiveness. The authors proposed that the default setting for our relationship to all species on Earth should be 'conservation', not inventing arguments to establish which species deserve to be saved on the basis of their perceived usefulness to human beings. The biggest threat faced by all of us who have conservation objectives at the heart of our actions is the widespread assumption that wildlife species and the environment are commodities purely for human beings to utilise. This unquestioned belief allows humans to pillage nature with impunity in order to harvest short-term financial gains.

In recent years, there has been an increasing recognition of the value of ecosystem services in achieving long-term sustainable development and human well-being, yet the value of individual species in maintaining these critical services has often been underrated or overlooked entirely. There are many examples of individual species' contribution to the well-being of humans: the anti-fouling treatment of boat hulls and adhesion technology, both derived from the study of blue mussels, which may result in massive fuel savings for marine vessels and advances in adhesives for medical applications; fiddler crabs helping mangrove trees grow larger, taller and thicker, helping to sequester more carbon from the atmosphere and helping to ease the climate-change problem.

This ecosystem recognition is extremely important for the health of our planet and its inhabitants, but the present approach has limitations. First, current conservation policies across the world incorporate the assumption that we already know the value of each species, which is, of course, far from the truth. All species are essential to maintaining healthy ecosystem services and need to be conserved while science continues to unlock the potential of species, such as a newly-described species of catfish in the Amazon basin whose unique gut bacteria can digest wood and may be help us manufacture paper using less energy. Second, it is difficult to assess the value of wild species without fully

9

understanding their properties and factoring in changes to the environment and society over time. When a species is lost or greatly reduced in an environment there are consequences. For instance, in the 1990s the Indian vulture was unintentionally poisoned, reducing its numbers by 90%; this resulted in an increase in feral dogs, which led to a greater occurrence of rabies across India and Pakistan. We may not know the role of most species in nature, but this does not make them unimportant; we should at least take the precautionary measure of not letting wildlife vanish just because we are unable to demonstrate what it can do for us.

Wild habitats are being lost around the world at an increasing pace, while the human population continues to grow and demand more resources. We – like all other life on earth – face pollution, deforestation, water shortages, flood, famine, unpredictable weather events, sea-level rise and the devastation of many ecosystems, causing what is being called 'the sixth great mass extinction'. This is not a fear for a distant future – we are already in this man-made period, witnessing extinction rates already many thousands of times higher than the background level.

The biggest challenge facing mankind is dealing with the consequences of climate change. If nothing is done to halt it, we shall lose a large percentage of the species on earth and countless human lives. Scientists have been warning us about this crisis for several decades, yet most politicians, and the general public, are paying little attention. If we can inform and educate the population about the facts, the consequences, and the ways we can all act to reduce the carbon emissions that contribute to climate change, then we stand a chance of mitigating the damage.

Habitat loss and species extinction also result from direct human actions such as poaching, mining, and planting non-native species. The challenge is to find ways of stopping destructive human actions, and getting governments and international conglomerates to act in the best interests of the planet rather than those of their voters or shareholders. We are faced by political weakness, short-sightedness and stupidity, based on fear, greed and corruption. Few members of the public are aware of the power of huge industries such as the fossil-fuel giants, major banks and financial institutions, nor of the meat industry. The problems can be overwhelming at times and we do not have time for complacency.

We already have the technology, the resources and the finances to overcome all the problems we face, even climate change. What is lacking is acknowledgement of the problems and the desire to make the necessary changes.

Believing people will care about the natural world because they see the beauty of wild places and wildlife on television clearly does not work well enough to bring about its protection. Because it looks so beautiful in documentaries, too many people think the natural world isn't doing too badly. The last fifty years have seen the rise of the 'blue-chip' documentaries (big budget films with superb cinematography concentrating on animal behaviour), and have also seen us inflict untold damage on the planet. This has mainly been unwitting damage: because the documentaries have not told the truth about the damaging effects of our current lifestyle, nor how we can start to fix things.

Some people say we already talk too much about conservation and climate change. But think of the saying: "If you keep on doing what you've always done, you'll keep on getting what you've always got." We are talking about the future of life on earth – the most important thing for any of us – and it should be shown and discussed on television (and other media) more widely. For example, as well as on news programmes, life-and-death conservation issues could be shown in a huge variety of ways: in quiz programmes, home-building features and magazine-format shows. We need to get into the audience's subconscious without them putting up immediate barriers.

The excuse that 'telling people the whole story turns them off or depresses them' is lame and old. We need to present the problems in a positive, pro-active, empowering and exciting way – above all we must make people care, and engage them. Massive budgets (multi-million dollars) are spent on wildlife films that are little more than eye-candy: disappointing, with weak stories and mentioning nothing of the real malaise of the natural world. Even worse, some of the major 'factual' channels – driven solely by ratings – broadcast films that are misleading and unethical.

There are a great many perils facing the natural world today. Since you are reading this book, we assume that concerns you and you want to do something about it. You may have a precise focus already: a local patch of forest under threat from developers, for example, plastic microbeads in the oceans, or climate change.

Film has become one of the most powerful tools for disseminating ideas and information to large numbers of people. It can also be a highly effective way of communicating with key individuals who are in a position to make changes. Studies have shown that television has become the main source of information for most people to learn about scientific research and discoveries.

Moving images can now be accessed in more ways than ever before: cinema/movie theatres; televisions in our homes; DVDs and Blu-Ray discs; via

11

the internet to our computers, tablets, phones and numerous other gadgets; in presentations given in person to key individuals, or screened in the field to small groups via digital projectors. A more unusual example is Ric O'Barry's method: strapping a flat-screen television to his chest – showing footage of the annual dolphin slaughter in Taiji, Japan (from the movie *The Cove*) – and gate-crashing an International Whaling Commission meeting where the scale of the slaughter was being played down. The moving images of the dolphin slaughter had a greater impact than any written report or impassioned speech would have done.

Ric O'Barry wanted to make a difference, and he succeeded, and he chose the medium of film to help him. This book is for anyone who wants to do the same. Whether you are a conservationist who is considering using film to help communicate your issues, a film-maker who wants to show the natural world as it really is, or an activist who wants to use film to create change in a direct way, this book aims to arm you with the tools you need.

It is a practical how-to guide, covering all stages of creating a film from the initial planning to reaching audiences and monitoring effectiveness. Although at times this book refers to the teams of people involved in film-making – especially when larger broadcasters and production companies are involved – it is also aimed at individuals, who may be just starting out in film-making, who will fulfil all these roles themselves.

We start with an in-depth guide to pre-production – everything that needs to be done and planned before a camera is even switched on. This is followed by a chapter on the all-important matter of raising funds for your production (however small or large in scale) and another on storytelling – how to ensure your film is something that will truly engage the viewer. Then we move on to the production stage, including choosing equipment, filming techniques and recording the sound. The section on post-production then discusses the editing of the movie and creation of the final product, before we look at how to reach your audiences and the often-overlooked matter of how to monitor whether your film has actually made a difference. The book also features a number of case studies in which we look at a variety of productions, film-makers, technologies and projects, all of which have used film to make a difference.

Film can be used to highlight the plight of a single animal or the future of all life on earth. To have the means to solve the problems facing this planet and yet not to use them is ridiculous in the extreme. Let's use film to help educate and empower everyone – from the general public to key politicians – about what the problems are and how they can be solved.

We need many more films to achieve this, and we must stop avoiding the full truth of what is happening in the natural world. Do we want future generations to think that we continued to show the public pretty pictures of business-as-normal in the natural world while species were becoming extinct just off-camera? Or do we want them to see that we were brave enough to face the truth and to educate creatively?

Make a film – make a difference!

Pre-Production Planning

As the saying goes, 'If you want to succeed at anything, create the conditions that are required for you to be successful'. Conservation film-makers are passionate about being successful in making a difference to the planet and the people who live on it. So how do we create the conditions that will give us the best chance of achieving our success?

In conservation film-making there are no set rules or regulations about the best way to succeed, or how to create the right conditions for yourself. You find a way that works for you, whether you are new to film-making or have been making professional films for years. Successful conservation film-makers are clear in what they want to achieve; this might be saving a rainforest, protecting diminishing tiger populations, supporting a community in its fight against mining concessions, or assisting law enforcers who are investigating the illegal trade in live animals. Millions of people are not interested in achieving any of these aims: they do not see the bigger picture of sustainability for the planet, and if they do see it, they don't care enough to take action. There are others, however, like you, who are prepared not only to stand up for what you believe in, but are willing to use their time, talent and resources to create a future very different from the one facing the human race at the moment.

Creating the right conditions for success; be honest and ask yourself ...

1. Why am I doing this?

There is a big difference between someone who wants to make a film and someone who wants to make a difference using film. The first person will be focussed on making a film no matter what the outcome, and the second person will consider who should make the film in order to have it achieve what is needed (which may be themselves, or a more experienced team). Neither answer is right or wrong, but the outcomes will be different.

2. How shall I make my film?

a) Guerrilla film-making – in which the film-maker picks up a camera and heads off to make a film. Anyone can do this. Passion can overcome lack of film-making technique, equipment and budget – as many guerrilla film-makers have shown. This approach provides creative freedom, immediate results, and the possibility of producing a film which may not gain support from traditional funding sources. It is a good way to learn 'on the job' if the objective is to provide a simple film with limited content and narrative structure for the end user. Remember, though, if the purpose is to create change, you will need to be sufficiently informed about the subject, and to communicate this well through your film, in order to achieve this goal. A film that fails to achieve this will be considered to be an entertainment and not a conservation film. Richard Brock (www.brockinitiative.org) is an example of a film-maker who just picked up a camera and got on with it, making many effective conservation films as a result. Guerrilla film-makers like him may find some of the advice in this chapter superfluous (indeed some of it is aimed at higher-budget, larger-team productions) but in any case it is best to consider all the implications of film-making before embarking on a project.

b) Low budget – in which the film-maker has some funding, (perhaps from an NGO) that allows the use of basic film-making equipment and permits some time to be spent filming the subject or species. Restricted budgets can encourage filmic invention, efficient scheduling and develop a strong editorial sense in the film-maker. These films, targeted at a particular audience, can be truly awe-inspiring, create substantial change in the world and – as a bonus – win film-making awards at the same time. Patrick Rouxel, Franny Armstrong and Shekar Dattatri are excellent exponents of low budget film-making.

c) Professional – in which the film-maker has a substantial budget to create a film for a specific audience designated by the funder or commissioner. This film will be a team effort with many talented people contributing their skills, with high production values. The film may be syndicated to other territories, increasing its opportunity to influence and inspire its audience.

3. Where do I begin?

Conservation films can be daunting to make, and there will be many excuses or reasons why they can't happen; the time isn't right, the political situation is uncertain, no-one will listen, the subject is too big for you to handle etc. Reasonable people will accept these arguments and sit back, waiting for a better opportunity to arise, more money to be given, permission to be granted; but conservation film-makers understand that we cannot afford the luxury of waiting nor, more importantly, allowing fear to hold us back. The only time in which we can act is the time given to us now, so we must begin with whatever skills, tools and resources we have and build on those as we go along … and begin at the beginning: pre-production.

Pre-production, fundamentally, means the organisation surrounding the practicalities of making your conservation film and the preparation for its success. Even the greatest story will struggle to reveal itself if your organisation fails – for example if the event you are hoping to film takes place at a different time, the crew doesn't arrive, your equipment is confiscated, the animals have moved to another location or you have run out of money. Pre-production is also about the attitude and approach you bring to your organisation, as the making of any film is likely to be difficult at times. Some difficulty is unavoidable, particularly when unexpected events interfere with well-organised plans, yet problems can be minimised by adopting the tips below:

Clarity

Discover what is needed, by whom and by when. You will need to assess what the most important elements of the film are, as these will take most of your time – locations, actors, contributors, animations, species behaviour etc. Examine each element and break it down into its component parts – what species you are filming, where it can be found, what conditions are required in order to film it, what health and safety issues must be highlighted. Is the behaviour you are seeking exhibited during the whole year or just at certain seasons? How likely are you to be able to see or film the species? The more detailed this analysis is, the better control you will have of even the smallest component of your production. The more control you have, the easier it is to be flexible and rise to the many challenges that are guaranteed to occur.

Communication

Communicate with everyone. There is a difference between communicating and speaking – one leaves people with knowledge enabling them to progress and the other leaves people with frustration and lots of questions. Communication begins with ascertaining what *you* need to know to fulfil the job you are doing. For example, a producer needs to have an understanding of all the constituent elements of the production, to ensure the film is delivered effectively. Therefore the producer will communicate with all key personnel, which may involve a lot of conversation if your film is a high-budget production (when the crew could include a production manager, researchers, key contributors, the accountant, a composer and the post-production team). Equally there may be just one other person if you are producing a low-budget or no-budget production. A camera operator will want to know limited, yet specific, detailed information such as what the story is, what the elements to be filmed are, where the film is being shot, what style and shooting format is required, the number of days for shooting etc. So the camera operator will communicate with the producer/director, production manager, possibly the editor and location fixer as well as any camera crew that are part of the team.

Every role involved in a production will need information that is specific and essential to that particular activity. Therefore you need to decide what information you require and which person(s) can provide it. Don't stop asking for information until you have everything you need, and don't guess. The effectiveness of the film and the reputation of the supporters and film-makers rely upon accurate information and excellent planning, the key to which is excellent communication. If communication within a team breaks down the consequences can be disastrous for the production and sometimes for the people involved. For example, an award-winning wildlife camera operator was employed by a broadcast producer who sent him to a site in the Arctic. The brief was to film birds. However when the operator arrived the local fixer had been given a different brief, to film polar bears. Unfortunately, the script had changed but the production team had omitted to tell the location team. The consequences for the location team were dire, as it had arranged for fuel to be dropped at the original location the previous year for its expedition in search of bears. Not only was the fuel in the wrong place, there was insufficient fuel to reach the location of the birds, so it was impossible to get the newly-scripted shots. The person who got the blame was the camera operator, for not delivering the shots!

Common Sense

Common sense is, beyond doubt, the greatest attribute a conservation film-maker can have. We inhabit a daunting, and often dangerous, world: the chance of unexpected occurrences is high. It is sensible to adopt the approach that 'if something can go wrong it probably will'. Being able to anticipate and mitigate problems will provide reassurance, and an opportunity to succeed if you have to fall back on a Plan B. Keep looking and listening for new obstacles or changes in your environment. Awareness of your situation and that of your team is imperative. This can range from simple observations – noticing that a camera is in a precarious position – to life-or-death warnings when wild animals or poachers are approaching.

Elements of Pre-Production

Research

The stories behind conservation films are often based on an issue or event that needs to be addressed or highlighted for an identified reason. A conservation film-maker is someone committed enough to accept the challenge of

17

communicating this story to the right audience. No matter how you decide to portray this communication stylistically, the basis of the film will be factual and your research needs to be highly accurate if your film is to be effective. It is often not easy to get good information given the corruption, self-interest and illegality of many activities at the heart of conservation issues;   but facts are power, and you need your film to be as powerful as it can be. It is worth being patient and thinking laterally to get to the truth; you may need to interview people you didn't have on your radar, scrutinise public records or follow up discrepancies in personal accounts. Whatever it is, you need to follow up the information until you are certain that you have managed to get to the heart of your story.

Searching for the Truth

a) The internet

For many people the primary and most valuable source of information is the internet, as long as they remember that information is not fact until it is verified. The internet is a great place to start researching your topic and you can consider a variety of options which will help you to clarify the key themes you want to explore, and support the discovery of your themes in depth. The bonus for internet users is freedom from constraints of time and space, but this is offset by the problems of establishing a writer's credentials and freedom from bias.

Sources:

- Search engines such as Yahoo, Bing, Google and Engine Colossus (which is linked to 148 countries)
- Directories that organise information and links, such as IPL2, infomine, Academic.info
- Websites devoted to particular topics eg internet directories for botany or stock photography
- Library sites like Amazon.com or Netflix.com.
- Personal websites
- News websites
- Podcasts and blogs
- Trade organisations
- Professional organisations
- Government websites
- NGO websites
- Social records
- Discussion forums

Using the internet:
- Use the appropriate research tools (Bing, Yahoo, Google etc)
- Use keywords relevant to the topic you are researching. Be specific and combine a number of your keywords; eg instead of searching for 'great apes Africa' enter 'Mountain Gorillas Bwindi National Park Uganda'. It can also be useful to enter alternative words eg when researching foreign films use the words 'movies' or 'shows' or 'screenings'
- Review several pages of results, not just the first listing on your search engine. Occasionally you can find valuable information on much later pages
- To help determine which website is credible attempt to verify the source of the information. Read the 'About Us' section of a website to discover information about the authors or organisation publishing the information and review the extension of the website in the address bar. If the website is overseen by an official body, in most cases it will be accurate eg '.edu' '.gov' '.org'
- Use as much up-to-date information as possible, because data can change and become outdated; eg statistics can vary, major events unfold rapidly. Check the date on your published information
- Examine the website for grammatical errors and broken links; these may indicate copying from another source that may not be legitimate
- Keep a copy of the internet sources you use, as you may need to return to the site and, more importantly, you may need to provide the provenance of your information

Avoiding errors:
- Author – who is the author, what are his or her credentials, has he or she written about this topic before, is he or she affiliated to a reputable organisation?
- Website – is it current, is the site date-stamped, are all the links up-to-date and working, who is the sponsor of the website?
- Accuracy – is the information factual, or opinion? Can you corroborate it through print sources? Is the source of the information clearly stated? Is the author's view impartial? Is the site error-free in terms of spelling and presentation?

b) Observation
Camcorder footage will appear to give a factual account of a physical situation. This can be misleading, since the view is dependent on the camera operator's decisions about where to point the camera. Be aware of this editorial potential when assessing footage you may want to use. On the other hand, a personal recording of an event or situation can be immensely powerful just because of its editorial position.

c) Personal Account

Interviews recorded on a camcorder will give you a valid account from a single perspective. This means that the person being interviewed cannot dispute that they have made those comments (however, this doesn't mean that the comments are necessarily true). The role of the interviewer will be to establish as much factual information as possible; however, if the interviewee quotes statistics you will need to check the alleged facts from other reliable sources like newspapers, scientific papers, industry figures etc before the film is edited.

Location

With your research completed, the location for your film will be clear; you will have chosen where it is to be, and why you want to go there. The next step is gaining permission from the landowner or building owner to allow you to work there.

Access: there are several factors to cover in order to obtain permission to film in particular locations. First you will need permission from the owner of the land, followed by permission from any other person or organisation associated with the land or premises. Access to roads or highways will need to be gained from the appropriate government bodies. It can sometimes be difficult to understand how many different people or authorities are involved with one location, so ensure that you have researched this fully. However, research doesn't always guarantee access: what if the location is an illegal goldmine or a controversial dam? Getting official permission to film at spots where you are not wanted will often be impossible; but you are strongly recommended to try. Conservation film-makers need to be making films not sitting in jail (or worse).

Permits: you may need to prove, legally, that you are entitled to be in a particular location at a particular time for the purpose of your declared film. A permit may be necessary to film a specific place or a specific species. To film endangered species many government and conservation bodies require you to have a licence authorised by an agreed regulatory body: in the UK this is a Schedule 1 licence to film birds that feature on the endangered species list.

Location Agreements: the legal documentation you require to enable your production to proceed at a specific location will usually be in the form of an agreement or a contract. Any such documentation should include all relevant information otherwise it may not be valid. This would include contact details of both parties, location address, date for filming, a statement of agreement by the owner giving permission for filming and details of what the filming may be used for, the address of the location, the terms under which the location can be used, details of insurance requirements and a clause ensuring copyright ownership of the filmed images rests with the production.

Special clauses: some locations have special requirements that will need to be taken into account, as they may impact your budget, schedule and the availability of logistical support and species. If, for example, you are filming in an animal sanctuary there will be requirements for biological control to protect the species from pathogens the crew might introduce. The main areas to include in your agreement would be site access, staff access, logistical support such as vehicles, accommodation, access to species, agreed filming times and activities and any security or health and safety considerations. In addition you will need to agree the fee for filming at the sanctuary and using the expertise of the staff.

Logistics: every location will have its own practical challenges, especially as many location owners are not familiar with filming techniques or practices. You should carefully assess the physical requirements of each of your locations: consider the size of a room, sound-proofing, eliminating or enhancing light. You may be in the middle of a public arena, or protected area, or in a space that cannot accommodate cameras easily (such as the cabin of a ship). You need to plan, in detail, how you will achieve the shots you require, and co-ordinate the logistics with the relevant people.

Interviewees and Presenters

Audiences respond to people in films. Stories can be successfully revealed through the viewpoint of a person audiences can relate to.

Interviewees
An interviewee may be the most appropriate person to reveal a particular element of your story. A subject expert, a company owner, a villager or a politician, all will provide an authenticity your audience will recognise. The challenge for a film-maker is that the interviewee is unlikely to have had any media training, and appearing on camera can be daunting. To help you get the best response from your interviewees here are some guidelines:

- Explain what the film is about, why it is being made and who will see it. You should then answer any questions that arise
- Explain why he or she has been chosen to do an interview and why his or her viewpoint is important (it might be a unique experience or the ability to highlight a perspective on the subject)
- Explain the nature of any other interviews to be included in the film, and mention other interviewees who may present opposing views in order that the film offers a balanced story

- Explain what the legal position is for the interviewee. The interviewee will be required to sign a document that gives you permission to use the interview in the film and edit the interview unhindered
- When you are ready to film, make your interviewee as relaxed as possible
- Have your questions ready in a form that is appropriate to the time and locations of the interview; in many communities it will not help you if you are waving a bunch of papers around
- Be connected to your interviewee, make eye-contact, ask your questions in a neutral way, adapt your method of questioning to the way your interviewee is responding; eg you may need to be reassuring or more energetic
- Be aware that some of your interviewees may not have English as their first language so they may need help in understanding your questions accurately
- Be fair to your interviewees; do not misrepresent them even if you do not agree with their views

Presenters

Good presenters are chosen for their ability to convey information to a chosen audience. Anyone can be a presenter as long as he or she is a good communicator and is appropriate for your story. Some of the most engaging and successful presenters have been those who are personally involved with the story being told. If your film is for a limited local audience it will be important for your presenter to speak the local language.

Checklist for interviewees and presenters:
- It is wise to book people as early as possible to ensure that they are available for your filming dates. Re-confirm arrangements with them close to those dates
- Payment will need to be clarified; think about costs associated with the interviewees, transport to your interview location, an overnight stay or a filming fee for presenters
- Does your interviewee need special arrangements; eg does he or she need anonymity or a translator?

Legal Framework

Setting up the legal framework for a conservation film can be daunting; yet even the shortest film, or the lowest-budget production, may contain elements that require legal protection or clarification. Conservation films can be controversial, so it is important to secure the legal position of your project before starting to film if possible. Legalities can be categorised as follows:

a) People

If you are making a conservation film that uses a person's image or voice you will need them to sign a **release form**. This gives permission to use their contribution in your film under the terms you have agreed. The form should be dated, and must clearly state that the person is waiving any rights that you choose to state explicitly in the agreement. Children appearing in your film will need a release form to be signed by a parent or other person authorised to grant permission. If you have a number of people appearing in your film who are unable to read or write, it can be confusing to work out which release form goes with which person. The answer is to request that the person being recorded states their name at the beginning or end of the recording and in this way you will have an accurate visual or audio record to match your legal paperwork.

A release form typically includes: the date of the agreement, the contact details of both parties, and the terms of copyright. The most useful and least restrictive copyright statement grants a film-maker 'full copyright in any visual, audio or written recording, in any media, throughout the world, in perpetuity'. It also includes the right for the film-maker to edit, modify or revise any of those contributions without penalty. Copyright should rest with the production company or the film-maker.

b) Crew

If your production requires a crew, its members will need a contract of engagement or a service agreement so that everyone understands what is required of him or her. The contract specifies the terms of the agreement between you and states all relevant information; eg the dates of engagement, a description of the services required, the payment due, any fixed hours of work, a clause identifying the copyright owner of the works created, any taxation required by law, public liability insurance if required, legal compliance with data protection, confidentiality if required, termination of contract clause including under what conditions this may take place and any miscellaneous additional terms you want to include. If you are working with animals you should include the ethical film-making guidelines for location crew.

c) Locations

The legal requirements for filming on location vary a lot from country to country; some countries are lenient with filming any subject you wish, yet others exhibit low tolerance towards activities they perceive as intrusion or even spying. To avoid problems, ensure that you are fully aware of permissions/guidelines for filming in the country where you wish to work. Find out if there are local guidelines to follow in addition to published national guidelines. Certain properties may wish to limit filming access to their premises, and the relevant owners or administrators will specify their own access rules.

- Museums may want to preserve their copyright on creative work, or prevent damage from flash photography or filming equipment
- Government buildings may be sensitive to a perceived security risk
- Restaurants may not want their customers inconvenienced, or reputational risk to their owners
- Sanctuaries need to restrict access to species because of to the threat from human diseases and disturbance
- Company offices may not want to be identified
- Airports have to mitigate possible security breaches
- Authorities responsible for public areas, such as streets, have to ensure the safety of all who use the space, including pedestrians and drivers
- Permission to film at particular locations may have be sought from each of the statutory bodies or organisations responsible for the area. Be careful: sometimes three or four different bodies may each be responsible for particular aspects of the land or property. If filming in a big city you can obtain permits from the local film commission and/or government departments. Statutory bodies will issue a standard filming permission or licence for the location, dates and conditions agreed. However, there will be times where no statutory agreement exists, so you will need to issue a licence to the location owners yourself. In this instance the licence to issue is a **Location Release Form.**

d) Licences

If your film contains any other non-original component such as music, stills or footage sourced from archives, you may require a licence from the copyright holders before any screening or publishing can take place. A licence typically includes:

1. Whom it is between: name(s) and contact details of all parties including email address if appropriate
2. Date of the agreement
3. The rights that are being granted:
- 'Theatric' allows the film to be screened to a fee-paying audience; eg in a cinema
- 'Non-theatric' permits a screening to non-fee-paying audiences, plus presentations and events
- 'Online' rights need to be qualified and the rights licensed should reflect the way you want to distribute your film. Depending upon how you want to reach your audience, you may require a licence for all online uses including downloadable and social media options
- 'Term' – the length of time the licence will be valid. If you can agree on ten years, or perpetuity, your film will have a good period of time to make a

difference. Most licences can be renewed on expiry but the cost is likely to have risen in the interim

- 'Territory' – if your conservation film is for a local audience or a specific part of the world you may need to licence just one country. The more countries (territories) you include in the licence, the greater the cost
- 'Non-exclusive' rights confirm that the copyright ownership of the material continues to rest with the creator, not the person who has obtained the licence.

e) Music

Finding music for a conservation film can be a creative and financial challenge. Fortunately for film-makers, some music producers generously offer rights to their music and sound effects – through designated libraries – for no payment. Alternatively, you may be able to obtain permission directly from the copyright-holder (if you can find them) or by contacting specialist companies who are legally entitled to assign copyright and collect royalty payments on behalf of composers and musicians. If your budget is limited it may be worth contacting music students, to enquire whether they would contribute their music to your production in exchange for the experience and the opportunity to showcase their talent.

f) Archive footage

There are many footage libraries worldwide that can be sourced via the internet. These companies are entitled to provide you with licensed footage for your production. The cost of archive footage varies greatly, depending how you use the material, how much footage you want, over what time and in which territories it will be viewed. There is often a premium rate for rare or newly-acquired footage, which can make accessing this material too costly for some productions. Additional opportunities exist for locating footage via individuals who have an interest or special access to the subject matter and who hold all copyright in the footage they have taken. This includes some wildlife camera operators, scientists or enthusiasts (see www.wildlife-film.com/companies/stock.html for many footage suppliers).

g) Stills

Some image libraries are generalist, and others may specialise in a particular genre such as historical images. Access to the images via the internet has made it easier for film-makers to search for, and download, the images they require. Specialist libraries can sometimes be more expensive than general interest libraries, since they need to maximise the financial reward from the limited interest in their images.

h) Distribution

If your film is being distributed to a third party you will need to negotiate the terms under which you allow them to screen or use your material. Professional distribution companies have access to sales markets worldwide (which increases the chances of your film's being seen in more territories), but they will charge for this service. Fees vary, but it is worth trying to negotiate a better deal with a company that seems keen to distribute your film. The basic fees will include a percentage of the sales achieved, the cost of distribution materials (tapes and translations) plus a marketing fee (to contribute towards publicity).

i) Endangered Species or Habitats

In many parts of the world protected species and habitats require a licence in order to obtain access and permission to film. Licences can be obtained from the appropriate Statutory Nature Conservation body.

j) Copyright Material

Copyright refers to the authors' (or creators such as writers, photographers, artists, film producers, composers and programmers) exclusive right to reproduce, prepare derivative versions, distribute copies and publicly perform and display their works. Copyright owners do not have to inform you that the content is copyrighted. Almost everything artistically created is copyrighted and its use will require permission from the creator. There are, however, some exceptions:

- Especially Licensed: there is a lot of media that has been made available for anyone to use, waiving the need to obtain direct permission from the creator. The most common licence is the 'Attribution' licence, which permits the use of the material for any purpose as long as the author is credited. The non-profit organisation Creative Commons offers a variety of attribution licences that creators apply to their work to make it available for public use
- Public Domain/Non-copyrighted works that are publically available are considered to be in the 'public domain'. This category includes works created before 1923, or where the copyright has expired, or where the work was created by a government
- Fair Use: different parts of the world have different copyright laws so it is useful to check the licensing rules that apply to the created work and the territory you are working in. 'Fair Use' is a provision in the copyright law in the USA that imposes limits and exceptions to the exclusive rights of authors. This means that copyright-protected media may be used without permission, purely for the purposes of criticism, comment, news reporting, teaching or research. If you invoke Fair Use you should always give full

credit to the author and use only a small amount of their material ... maybe five seconds of film.

- Certain material – such as facts, single words, titles or short expressions (other than Trade Marks) – cannot be copyrighted

k) Misrepresentation

Viewer trust is especially important for conservation films; if your film is to have the impact and influence you desire it must be accepted as being an accurate representation of facts and events. Any reconstructions of real events must be done accurately, and will need to be identified as such on screen in order to avoid misleading the viewer. Similarly, the filming of captive animals or computer-generated animal behaviour should be declared for the same reason. The editing process will inevitably condense events that have occurred over a period of time but this must not give a distorted view of reality. Ultimately truth must not be sacrificed for the sake of creating a more entertaining film; it is never acceptable to present something as true that didn't happen, unless the viewer will clearly understand that it is fiction.

l) Criminal activity

It is imperative that you consider very carefully before choosing to undertake filming activities (eg for the purpose of exposing illegal operations) that put you at risk of being arrested or charged with an offence. Conduct extensive research and preparation and take legal advice. It is particularly important not to become involved in inciting others to commit a crime.

Travel

- Many airlines will give special consideration (cheap, flexible flights and additional baggage allowance) to conservation film-makers if they are working with an NGO
- If you book accommodation make sure it is fit for purpose: does it need to have space for camera equipment; is it easily accessible for heavy kit without a lift; does it have power to charge batteries?
- Booking vehicles, unseen, needs particular attention. Confirm that you have the correct size of vehicle for the crew, equipment and data storage. What is the insurance cover? Can you film effectively from the vehicle?
- Check your crew has up-to-date documentation, visas, medical certificates and passports
- Small camcorders can be taken through customs without restriction but larger cameras will need a 'carnet'. This is a document to prove that you are not exporting the equipment when you leave the country, nor importing it when you return. It is important to establish (from the relevant customs

27

authorities) whether your equipment needs this protection, as you do not want it impounded at customs

- If you can, get a letter of invitation from a local, established, NGO that states that you are travelling with your equipment (itemised) to work on a project with them – it may save you a lot of time, and spare you bribery demands and extortionate customs fees. In many parts of the world it is also helpful to have a local official meet you at an airport, to assist the passage of your equipment into the country and prevent it being held at customs – possibly for days or even weeks
- Local transport can often be of poor standard, and should be checked for safety whenever possible.

Insurance

Insurance is an important part of film-making and at the very least you should consider cover for health and safety, crew and equipment. Unfortunately, conservation film-making by its nature often involves working in dangerous situations. Judge the risk of each element, and balance possible loss against the potential benefits of making the film.

Factors that should be considered for insurance:

- Crew: it is important to ensure that everyone associated with your film is suitably skilled at the work they are being engaged to do. This will reduce both your policy premium and the risk of problems occurring during your filming
- Travel requirements throughout the shoot
- Equipment failure or theft: even the most basic filming equipment costs money, so protecting your investment against loss or damage is important. Note that loss of equipment caused by theft from unattended vehicles or fraud is usually excluded under a filming policy
- Cancellation of filming, loss of rushes (if you are making a film with a reasonable budget for a commissioner and are contractually obliged to deliver the film by an agreed time)
- Weather cover if climatic conditions are an important element of your film
- Public liability will cover your filming in the event that a person gets hurt or property gets damaged
- Medical cover and repatriation.

Health and safety

Ultimately this is the personal responsibility of the producer or film-maker, who will have to live with the emotional, financial and legal impact if someone is seriously injured or killed during their production. In order to achieve high standards of health and safety everyone involved in the production will need to play their part by recognising and acknowledging their own role in the process. This will require good communication, organisation and planning throughout the production period.

In general:

- Satisfy yourself that everyone involved is sufficiently skilled in the tasks they are required to undertake.
- Ensure that you have all the specialist advice and necessary equipment in order to keep everyone safe especially if they are involved with dangerous activities like rope-work or underwater diving. Have the equipment double checked by an expert immediately before the filming
- Hazards – anything that can cause harm to people, species, property or habitats – will need to be identified in advance, and safety measures be put in place to mitigate all anticipated problems
- Make sure that everyone involved in the filming is fully briefed on all safety considerations and health-protection before filming
- Create a risk assessment analysis before filming, for every location, activity and species you will encounter during your production
- Report any incident to the appropriate authority and then to the insurers
- Monitor health and safety throughout the production process, not just at the beginning
- Have a detailed plan for any emergencies and ensure this is communicated to everyone concerned.

Health preparation before the filming is fairly straightforward:

- Ensure the crew members are physically fit for the specific tasks they will need to undertake, and the location(s) where they will be working. Extreme temperatures, humidity, rough terrain and lack of shelter are just some of the challenges that may arise
- Disease is a risk and needs to be handled appropriately. Precautions include appropriate injections, using anti-bacterial hand wash, face-masks, carrying an adequate supply of any medication required (in case the schedule changes, or your return trip is delayed), basic medication for ailments like diarrhoea, cuts and scratches
- Clean water can be hard to find in many parts of the world, so purification tablets and kits are often vital. The standard, common-sense, precautions apply: boil your water, and don't have ice or ice cubes in drinks

- Check and follow all the World Health Organisation advice for your filming locations. This relevant and highly effective information will ensure you are up-to-date with any necessary measures
- Basic First Aid training for everyone on location is important, and could be a life-saver not just for the film-making team but also for communities that you may be working with in the field
- Wherever you are filming, be it a city or a remote desert, make sure that you have up-to-date details of how to contact health practitioners, and have a plan for reaching them urgently if necessary. This is especially important if you are working in remote regions and inaccessible places. Camera crew members have died because they couldn't reach help in time

Safety is, of course, vital for any production. The only way to anticipate many hazards is to do a full risk-assessment for every location and filming event. This will entail identifying each risk, how likely it is to happen, and planning to implement every mitigating action you can think of – especially before filming wildlife or working in dangerous situations.

- Look for hazards that are significant
- Consider who may be at risk from the hazards
- Consider the chance and severity of harm that each hazard may cause, and judge how likely it is to happen on a scale of low, medium or high
- Establish how to prevent, reduce or mitigate the harm
- Put the findings into a risk assessment form
- Give the risk assessment to all those who may be involved: eg police, local authorities, communities
- Conservation film-making often involves an unfolding story: the film-maker has to be flexible because situations can change at short notice. In this instance, you will need to circulate a 'live' risk assessment during your production, which tracks how any risk has changed and modified the assessment you originally provided.

Some safety measures to consider including in your production:
- Security or safety protection – specialist training or protection, provided by personnel trained in coping with the particular hazard you are mitigating, whether it be a war zone, disease area, mountainous region or dense jungle
- Vehicle maintenance and 4x4 training could be useful if travelling to remote regions
- Underwater filming requires camera operators who are up-to-date with international diving requirements and have the required diving qualifications
- Secret or surreptitious filming can be a powerful journalistic tool: material obtained this way may be the only independent account of the wrongdoing it captures. Secret filming has changed working practices, closed facilities

and led to changes in the law. As technology changes, so too does the opportunity to obtain images in this way. This must be handled with due responsibility, in order to protect any innocent individuals involved and to ensure that the account is completely accurate. Consider who will be carrying the equipment, who will accompany them, what safety arrangements can be made to protect them, what equipment will be used and how is will be carried, what the circumstances of the secret filming are, what evidence there is of wrongdoing, and whether the images could be obtained in any other way.

The Team

You may think you know the size of your team; perhaps you are a one-man band, or you may be a small team of two to five people, or even more. However, your team is always bigger than you think it is when, you take into consideration all the people connected to your production. This extended team includes the people you contact for your research, any interviewees, organisations, sanctuaries, funders, and anyone concerned with controlling your accounts or distributing your film. In their own way all these people contribute to the end result and should be treated accordingly. Conservation film-making is a form of film-making that does not suit everyone, so choose your team carefully: they will need personal qualities not required by some other film genres. What you are seeking is people with personal conviction, flexibility to think on their feet, sensitivity to local customs and communities, endurance, comprehension of the issues you are exploring, experience in how to protect themselves in uncertain circumstances, plus the traditional skills of creativity and film-making knowledge. Your film may need to include a person or a group of people who can source the funding, organise the production (including legal, accounts and health and safety), operate a camera, record sound, edit images and distribute the final film (including any publicity that may help you to create the end result you are aiming at).

The Budget

Since the advent of digital video technology, the means of creating films has become more democratised. Film-makers can shoot, edit, create the sound and music, and mix it all together on a home computer. This individualised method of producing films can be highly cost-effective. The other end of the financial scale could be a film that requires international locations, large numbers of crew members, a shooting schedule that lasts for months, technically challenging computer-generated images and a famous narrator. So how do you establish how much your film will cost?

Your budget needs to be accurately constructed to reflect the script you are shooting. This is the point where the financial realities of your creative ambition are highlighted and analysed, to establish whether your funding is adequate. At this important stage in your production you may need to have flexibility of approach, in order to find ways to match your available funding to the story you intend to tell. If you have a funding shortfall your options are either to find more money, or reduce costs -- or possibly both. For example, can you adapt your storyline; is it possible to lose a location; is there a cheaper source of equipment; can anyone provide time, skill, resources or equipment for nothing? Making a conservation film is an unpredictable process and you should include a contingency factor of at least five percent of the budget as a safety measure.

If you do need to save money, or stretch your budget, you will need to do deals everywhere and accept any support offered from local sources or appropriate companies and individuals. Conservation film-makers, however, should be careful not take advantage of NGOs or sanctuaries which have very limited resources and, because they are keen to highlight a situation or issue, are vulnerable to exploitation by production companies. These dedicated people need support – most importantly financial support – in order to continue the vital role they are contributing. The least film-makers can do is to pay them for the services they provide: eg access to stories, research, local contacts, species and habitats, staff, vehicles and accommodation. It may also be possible to provide an NGO with copies of any film produced at their facilities, and to add a link to their work on an associated website.

Be prepared to pay for these elements of a budget:

1. Development
- Research
- Recce costs

2. Production
- Crew fees
- Travel and subsistence
- Translators
- Equipment, camera, stock and sound
- Car or vehicles and fuel
- Permits
- Location fees
- Stills
- Consultants or experts
- Inoculations
- Training required

- Security
- Bank charges for currency conversion

3. Post-production
- Editor
- Transcription of interviews
- Narration, recording suite
- Archive footage or stills
- Music
- Graphics if required, including titles and credits
- Sound mix
- Transfers and conversions

4. Distribution
- Copies of the film
- Supporting information, brochures, questionnaires, monitoring
- Local facilitators or educators for screenings
- Local screening costs, blackout materials
- Travel for screening programmes, road-shows
- Website
- Reports to funders

Recce

The purpose of a recce is to visit the location or premises where you are about to film, meet the people who will assist you, discover any logistical problems, establish potential filming positions and gain all the information you will require to produce the film. Some films have to be shot undercover, but even then a lot of information can be gained before the actual filming. On your recce you will need to establish the following:

- Where you are going to film – exact locations, what camera positions are possible, the challenges for sound recording, any safety considerations, availability of the site
- What you are filming at the location, and if there are any specific associated timing issues – species, habitat, events, tides, monsoons
- Who will be filmed at the location, under what conditions and when they are available – contributors, experts, presenters
- Logistics – whereabouts of ATM, food supplies, accommodation; where to get electricity for batteries, where to rent vehicles. You will need to establish the best route to your location and determine what environmental challenges exist

- What equipment will be necessary – camera, lenses, sound, lights, tracks or dollies, data storage; how will all this be transported to the location, and protected during filming?
- Local travel arrangements – any changes to published transport schedules, availability of local transport, length of required journeys
- Permits/fees required
- Local customs – sensitivities, festivals, beliefs

Schedule

Even when a budget is confirmed, scheduling a shoot can be difficult. You will need to identify all the elements in the film, to determine how and when to allocate the production budget. Be realistic when scheduling your shoots, allow for weather conditions, local events, inexperienced interviewees, setting up equipment and local logistical challenges. Breaking down your shoot into a daily timetable should confirm:

- How many days it will take to film your story
- When each filming day needs to happen (some events only happen at certain times of the day or year)
- When your interviewees or consultants are required (sometimes people have other commitments)
- When your equipment is required
- When to book travel and accommodation
- The dates for the film crew
- When to book vehicles
- The dates for location bookings such as sanctuaries and venues
- Dates for filming species or habitats
- Dates for post-production
- A date for delivery of the final film
- Organisation of distribution

A diary/spreadsheet will be your best friend when you are scheduling: it will help you to choose the best dates for each element of the filming, from development to delivery, and help you to avoid days that may be problematic, such as national holidays or busy travel times. It may be helpful to identify each location or element of the film by highlighting it in a different colour. This will give you clarity about the requirements of each element and assist you in matching your budget to the schedule you have created. It is easier to recognise where to make any financial cuts or alterations when the various elements are clearly laid before you. It will also make it easier for you to adapt your schedule when you are required to change elements.

Funding

Funding films in any genre is hard, but conservation films are especially challenging. Not only do you have to seek the budget you need, but you also need to ensure that your funding source has ethical credentials that will support the objectives of your film, not undermine them. There is a number of ways to approach funding your film, both traditional and non-traditional; reviewing all the options available will allow you to create a funding plan to match the type of film you want to create. Here are some of the most popular routes for obtaining funding:

Self-Funded Films

Passion, dedication and commitment can produce the most amazing films on a very low budget. A basic kit of camera, tripod, microphone and laptop has given film-makers the opportunity to provide education, inspiration and resources to communities around the world. Film-makers who are working under these financial constraints need all the ingenuity and creativity they can muster. They also draw on support from their wider network: friends, contacts in the field and specialist groups. Their films do not have to reach professional standards but they do have to carry the right message in the right way to the right people.

Crowdfunding

There are thousands of people in the world who are passionate about the same things that you are, and are prepared to partner you on your film-making journey by putting their hard-earned cash into your film. Whether it is a tiny amount of money, or thousands of pounds or dollars, they are all investing in your dream, effectively becoming part of it. As with everything in life, this has its positives and its negatives. It is estimated that sixty percent of projects fail to obtain significant funding through crowd-funding. The forty percent success rate is enough encouragement for many film-makers to put time and energy into this potential funding route. So, it is worth learning from them what works and what to avoid; and when you are successful, be prepared for other learners to contact you for advice.

To begin with, ensure that you have your film project fully defined before you start to ask for money; ie have your final shooting script completed, agreement for any experts you want to appear, permission from locations. In addition, create a press kit that includes the CVs of all key people involved, a synopsis of the story, a show-reel if you have one, a distribution plan revealing how your film will reach the people who need to see it, an explanation of how you are going to monitor any change your film may instigate and, finally, an outline of what the funders will receive in return.

A scale of returns, in proportion to donations, will be helpful and may extend generosity! Rewards can range from a DVD of the final film, or monthly reports charting changes on the ground, or attending a première (maybe with the community where the film was produced).

Here are some tips that successful crowd-funding users have offered:

- Allow at least six months for the pre-launch process, to give time for interest to build in your film. There will not be enough time to develop support for your film if you begin to publicise it after you have posted your project on a crowdfunding site

- You will already know, from your research, what your audience is and therefore what genre of film will most appeal to it.

- Documentaries based on emotional and political stories are the films with the most funding potential.

- The response you receive will directly relate to the amount of work you put into creating a really exciting pitch and finding the right potential investors to pitch to

- Your website and blog should support the project with engaging, appropriate images and a short video of your pitch. Add an active presence on Twitter and Facebook and you are ready to go. Ideally you will post something daily, but if this isn't possible aim for weekly as a minimum

- Collect email addresses as widely as you can, then use free plugins and online tools to send bulletins to everyone on your list – especially when you have an exciting update to share

- Call everyone you know and ask them to call everyone they know and so on; this creates a community of people who are prepared to spread the word around. Ask your followers how they found out about your project and what captured their interest. There are other sites that can get the word out for you, so it may be worth looking at:

- o **ThunderClap** is designed to build momentum during a pre-launch of projects
- o **PitchFuse** allows you to track interest in your project, accumulate followers, analyse page-views, collect emails and receive comments before you launch, so you can adapt your pitch to make it even more powerful
- o **CF4ALL** gives projects crowd credits based on the interest generated in your project, and showcases projects with the most credits on the CF4ALL website
- o **CrowdfundingPR** gives the opportunity to create free press releases for your project. Paid upgrades allow you to blog and connect with other bloggers, journalists, friends and supporters
- o **LaunchRock** or **Prefundia** gives you a tool to create a pre-launch landing page for collecting emails of potential investors prior to your actual launch

- Be honest with your investors; the measure of success for your film will be in the results it produces and the change it will make on a local/global scale. You may also make money from distributing it to commissioners, or having a theatrical release; but conservation films do not have profit as their primary goal

- Create a realistic crowdfunding budget and determine the level of return for particular amounts of funding. As you approach your funding goal, increase the level of investment required for the return you offer. People who have invested early on have taken more risk with you and should be rewarded at a higher level than later investors. Levels of investment suggested by Film School Online are as follows:

  - o £1–£24: considered a donation with no return
  - o £25–£50: investor receives a DVD of the finished film
  - o £51–£250: the investor receives a credit at the end of the film
  - o £250–£999: you can be creative at this point ... reports and photographs from the field; letters from a community; attendance at a local première etc

- Be professional in your approach at every level: the website; the contact emails; setting up a business bank account etc.

- Decide on the appropriate crowdfunding website for your project, checking its terms and deductions. You will be entering an agreement that is a fairly new concept, and is currently being examined for regulatory control by statutory bodies such as taxation offices. The first consumer-protection lawsuit has recently been filed for a Kickstarter fundraiser who failed to deliver on their project after raising $25,000

Popular sites at present are:

a) **Kickstarter** (www.kickstarter.com) launched in April 2009 with a $1,000 project and hosted its first million-dollar project in 2012. So far it has raised over a billion dollars to help visionaries like you. Kickstarter won't charge those who have pledged to support you until your reach your target. Given that it has only a 39% success-rate for funding film projects, Kickstarter will accept projects with only tangible products, rather than nebulous aims such as 'social impact'. Therefore think carefully about how you pitch your film and what tangible results or products you are aiming to deliver. Kickstarter has high traffic volumes, which is great for profile and building your community; but you will lose all your funding if you do not reach your target (this is where your realistic budgeting comes in). Owing to the popularity of the site your project will be competing with many others for the same funders; but when they do find you, and want to support your film, it is fairly easy for them to do so. Amazon – which charges for processing credit-card payments – collects the payment, and deducts the first fee from your funding. The second fee deducted is from Kickstarter, which takes 5% if you reach your target amount. Both these fees should be factored into your funding goal

b) **IndieGoGo (**www.indiegogo.com) specialises in creative projects like films, and has the additional benefit of allowing you to seek part ('partial' means 'biased') funding and does not require you to set a funding goal. The downside is that it is currently smaller than Kickstarter. Fees are different for different plans, and investors pay through PayPal (which charges significant commission) or bank transfers. Indiegogo has Fixed Funding and Flexible Funding as well as Non-Profit Funding. Fixed Funding works on a specified goal basis; if you don't reach the goal you get nothing and they do not charge a fee. Flexible Funding allows you to keep any amount you raise regardless of whether or not you reached your target, but IndieGoGo takes 9% if you do not reach your goal and 4% if you do

c) **RocketHub** (www.rockethub.com) has higher fees than other sites but offers a larger international range than some others as well as flexible funding options

d) **Micro ventures** (https://microventures.com) isn't a crowd funding-site but it is a venture capital organisation, an online service that is open to the public and connects start-ups with interested angel investors. It screens you on several levels of due diligence then finds you some angels. This will cost you $100 to submit, $250 for due diligence checks and 5–10% of the total raised; so it's for financially ambitious projects only

e) **Crowdtilt (**https://www.tilt.com) is a bit different from other crowdfunding schemes in that small groups with small goals can benefit. Crowdtilt helps non-profit groups and charges them 2% of the funding raised once their goal is reached – or 'tilted'

f) **GoGetFunding** (gogetfunding.com) is for all-purpose crowdfunding

g) **Fundable** (https://www.fundable.com) allows you to build a page about your project on their website, and collect secure online donations for any amount

h) Advertise on **Craigslist** (craigslist.co.uk) and offer a credit at the end of your film.

i) **Cinecrowd** (cinecrowd.com) provides an opportunity for film-makers to pitch their ideas to the public; anyone can contribute to a film and help to make it happen. You will need to offer gifts in exchange, but if your film does not reach its goal the money is refunded to the funder.

Grants

There are many national programmes which provide grants for film-making, but you will have to make sure your application rises above the many other applications that they receive. Therefore you will need to write a very professional document that reveals your expertise and passion for your project while conforming to the guidelines of the application forms. There are sources – such as the National Science Foundation's *Guide to Proposal Writing* – to guide you in how to make effective grant applications, but at a basic level they all require a detailed proposal of your project, a budget, a schedule and a reporting structure.

If you would like help or training to assist with your funding applications these organisations may be helpful:

o **The Documentary Film Group** provides training for documentary film-makers
o **Grierson Awards** celebrates documentaries worldwide that have made a significant contribution to the genre. The Grierson Trust runs education and mentoring initiatives
o **Skillset** in the UK

o   **Women in Film and Television** UK.

Consider the following when applying for grants:

o   Don't overlook small grants, they can contribute to a particular element of your project
o   Research grant-funding opportunities in your area or at the International Documentary Association's website (www.documentary.org).

Potential international sources for grants:

a) **Channel 4 BRITDOC Foundation** (britdoc.org) for the UK and the rest of the world. It exists to nurture independent documentary film-makers

b) **DocHouse** (www.dochouse.org/online/resources): the UK is considered across the world to be a centre of excellence for documentary film-making but does not have a permanent centre dedicated to the promotion of documentaries. DocHouse attempts to address this lack by promoting public access, encouraging the use of documentaries in education, and bringing together the media, educators, public and students

c) **The Paul Robeson Fund** (www.documentary.org/content/paul-robeson-fund-independent-media) provides grants of $2,000–$15,000 for documentary films about social issues

d) **Sundance Documentary Fund** (www.documentary.org/calendar/sundance-documentary-fund) assists the development of films addressing social issues

e) **MacArthur Foundation Documentary Film Grant** (www.filmproposals.com/macarthur-foundation-documentary-film-grant.html#) offers grants for film-makers to produce high-quality, professionally produced, serious, fact-based journalism for television, radio or the web. The supported films inform and educate the audience about important and under-reported topics, provide balance and accurate information, and encourage global conversations and interactivity

f) **Bertha BRITDOC Connected Fund** (britdoc.org/real_funds/bertha-britdoc-connect-fund) for outreach and engagement

g) **Bourse Auteur de Documentaries** (fondation-jeanluclagardere.com/bourses/presentation/auteur-de-documentaire) The Jean-Luc Lagardère Foundation

40

h) **CBA Worldwide View** (worldview.cba.org.uk) project development

i) **Cinereach Grants and Awards**
(documentaries.about.com/od/introtodocumentaries/p/Cinereach.htm)

j) **Cinergia** Fondo de Fomento al Audiovisual de centramerica y el caribe
(www.cinergia.org)

k) **Ford Foundation** (www.fordfoundation.org/grants)

l) **Fundation (is that right?) Alter-Cine Documentary Film Grants**
(www.altercine.org/html/en/programme-de-bourses.php)
Africa/Asia/Latin America

m) **Goteborg International Film Festival Fund**
(https://acige.wordpress.com/2010/08/16/goteborg-international-film-festival-fund-giff/)

n) **Hot Docs Blue Ice Film Documentary Fund**
(www.hotdocs.ca/funds/hot_docs_blue_ice_film_documentary_fund_guideline
s) for African film-makers

o) **Hubert Bals Fund** (https://www.iffr.com/en/about/hubert_bals_fund)

p) **IDFA Jan Vrijman Fund** (realscreen.com/2012/03/22/jan-vrijman-fund-names-20-grant-recipients) for developing countries

q) **ITVS International Call** (itvs.org/funding)

r) **LEF Foundation Moving Image Fund**
(www.lef-foundation.org/DefaultPermissions/NewEngland/tabid/160/
Default.aspx)

s) **Mama Cash** (www.mamacash.org) Netherlands

t) **National Geographic All Roads Film Grant**
(www.humanities.ufl.edu/funding/march-faculty-national-geo-film.html)

u) **One World Media Fund** (oneworldmedia.org.uk/)

v) **Prince Claus Fund** (www.princeclausfund.org/en/programmes/grants-collaborations) for culture and development

w) **PUMA** Creative Catalyst Awards – International Development Fund (britdoc.org/)

x) **SANAD** Development and Post-production Fund – Abu Dhabi Film Festival (www.abudhabifilmfestival.ae/en/sanad-fund/about)

y) **Screen Institute Beirut Film Fund**
(www.screeninstitutebeirut.org/filmfund.html)

z) **World Cinema Fund** – Berlin
(www.berlinale.de/en/branche/world_cinema_fund/wcf_news/WCF_News.ht
ml)

Other useful international grant funders:

o   Shaw Media – Hot Docs Funds Canada (www.shawmedia.ca)
o   TFI Documentary Fund – Tribeca Documentary Institute
    (https://tribecafilminstitute.org/programs/detail/tfi_documentary_fund)
o   Fledgling Fund – New York (www.thefledglingfund.org)
o   The Manuel Rivera-Ortiz Foundation for Documentary Photography and
    Film (mrofoundation.org)
o   Rockefeller   Foundation   Grants   (www.rockefellerfoundation.org/our-
    work/grants)
o   UK Media Desk (www.creativeeuropeuk.eu)
o   Visions Sud Est Switzerland
    (www.visionssudest.ch/?index&language=en)

Non-Profit Organisations

Many non-profit organisations are willing to engage with film-makers, and to support projects because they are interested in promoting the message of the film; this is just the start of the benefits for them. Alongside the environmental or social change that your film will encourage, non-profit organisations are able to offset their donation against tax so the return is immediate and risk-free. For first-time film-makers charitable support is a legitimate way to secure funding. Non-profit organisations recognise that a lot of the work done on independent films is essentially volunteer time, donated to complete a worthwhile project, hence they may offer the film-maker support in varied ways, eg accommodation on site, expertise on the subject of the film, or access to restricted areas. The downside is that non-profit organisation or charity funding levels will be necessarily limited. The USA has strong non-profit support for film-makers who can apply to geographic programmes such as the Minnesota Independent Film Fund and to funds set up specifically for recognised groups like the National

Black Programming Consortium and the Fund for Jewish Documentary Film-making. Non-profit organisations may not be able to contribute directly to the funding of your film, but they may be able to raise the money from their own supporters.

Government Funding

Many nations now have attractive tax and investment incentives for film-makers. Europe's MEDIA programme has over twenty programmes for media and film-makers; they are oversubscribed, but be confident – someone has to be successful. In the UK the government allocates millions of pounds every year for British Film via the BFI, but other government departments such as Defra, and the DFID are also worth investigating. In the USA government funding can be accessed via the US Fish & Wildlife Department. Governments worldwide have departments for the Environment and Wildlife, many of which have requirements for outreach, education and communicating solutions to local issues; so films relating to key issues of concern can be very welcome.

Corporate Social Responsibility

With the growth of consumer scrutiny and demands from governments for companies to establish clearer and stronger ethical practices, many large corporations are seeking ways to prove their corporate social responsibility (CSR). Research into the companies' businesses, their customer-bases, the products they sell and any legal action they have been involved with is required in order to establish whether or not you choose to support their CSR and avoid just 'green-washing' (when a company or organisation spends more time and money claiming to be 'green' through advertising and marketing than actually implementing business practices that minimize environmental impact). There are plenty of companies who genuinely want to contribute to improving the environment or human condition, so it is worth seeking them out.

Prepare a full business plan that includes an introduction outlining why they should invest in your film project, how they would benefit from being your partner, a concise outline of the project including the schedule, a detailed budget and any opportunities you can create whereby the company employees may become involved – and present the information in a professional way. It is a lot of work; you may find it helpful to ask a friendly business leader to review your documents before you send them to your designated company. The bonus for you, if the business accepts your proposal, is that the funding is guaranteed, you may access their public relations teams or their website to promote your film, and help you maximise any results you are aiming for.

43

High Net-Worth Individuals

Does the subject of your film stir the passion of anyone who is seeking to donate to a cause they believe in? People who have an altruistic outlook on life can be given the opportunity to make a difference by donating to, or fully funding, your film. If you find a wealthy individual who echoes your commitment to make a tangible change, ensure that you respect any terms and conditions they may have. Such funders are often sensitive about privacy, so respect the terms under which they engage with you, and treat them as your partner. This means discovering what they want to achieve by funding you – you might keep them informed of progress, invite them to any première, provide an accounting record detailing how you spent their money, acknowledge their contribution in an appropriate way, or provide a full report itemising the success of the project. If your funder is happy with the difference you have made together, he or she may wish to continue to fund you.

Broadcasters

The media world for broadcasters is expanding all the time; cable, satellite, mobiles, video-on-demand, subscription video-on-demand are alternative distribution channels that may purchase existing programming (known as 'acquisition') or fund new films (known as 'commission').

Acquisition: if you have a film or series that would fit with existing programming on a broadcast channel, or on a variety of channels, you can make your films available for sale to the broadcast networks. This process of distribution requires up-to-date knowledge of what films are sought by international broadcasters in each territory worldwide and how much they will pay for screening the films. To gain this knowledge takes a lot of time, knowledge and research, so most film-makers consider using a distributor to do the work. Distributors will sell your film(s) and take a percentage of the income, plus a fee for any viewing materials (DVDs etc) and public relations activities.

Commission: there are channels with dedicated programming for wildlife, environment and social issues. Well-established wildlife and environment series are usually allocated in-house to the broadcaster's production unit or to external production companies who are known to have delivered similar content. But there are various possibilities even for newcomers.

Getting a Commission: Opportunities

1. If you have a strong story that fits with the audience profile and format of a particular programme strand, it may be worth considering joining forces with

one of the established production companies. You would need to be clear about what you are providing (story, permissions, key contributors, possibly part funding) and what your position is to be on the production; but if you can negotiate successfully this route may be the funding opportunity that your film needs.

2. From time to time various schemes are set up by broadcasters and other organisations that produce a series of short films. Keep an eye out for announcements about new schemes (for example via *Wildlife Film News* – www.wildlife-film.com).

3. One broadcaster which is expanding its content in the area of wildlife and the environment is Netflix, the cable and satellite network which recently funded *Virunga* (the feature-length documentary) so successfully. Netflix also acquires films.

4. Another avenue to explore is local television, which is expanding its audience figures in many countries. In the UK alone there are currently nineteen local television networks, which have very tiny budgets but are content-hungry – so you have the opportunity to offer to provide them with films on local wildlife or environmental subjects.

5. Europe has a well-established route for obtaining commissions from broadcasters. A number of the major wildlife broadcasters give you the opportunity to send in proposals online; Discovery is one. There is no restriction on how many broadcasters you initially send your proposal to, but you will have more chance of success if the proposal is matched to an identified 'need' the broadcaster has. Many broadcasters hold meetings with production companies, and have open discussions at festivals, in order to communicate what their current programming 'need' is. Once you have completed your research and fully understand what a broadcast commissioner is seeking, you can write your film idea and turn it into a 'proposal'. Recommendations for film proposals vary from broadcaster to broadcaster, but generally they have a few recommendations in common.

Writing a Proposal:

1. Keep the proposal to one page if at all possible

2. The film should have an engaging title

3. Introduce the core idea in a concise paragraph at the head of the proposal. Consider each word carefully: it has to grab attention and bring the idea to life

45

4. Images are powerful additions to your proposal, but they must be relevant

5. Create short paragraphs, setting the scene/location, outlining the story, revealing the reason why the public may want to watch this film

6. If you have a special presenter, contributor or camera-operator, include their details

7. Each broadcaster has its own brand style, which is evident in the format of programmes they produce and the way they graphically present themselves. Consider emulating this style in your proposal; it will show the commissioner you have done your homework and appreciate the brand

Once your proposal is in the hands of a commissioner, the first questions you are likely to be asked are about the budget: there is little value using time exploring a potential production that is too expensive for the particular broadcasting channel. The other pertinent questions will focus on your schedule, your crew (a polite way of examining your skill level and your ability to produce the film you are proposing), your location logistics and the species or issue you are filming. Expect your proposal to be challenged by the commissioner, and accept this as valuable insight and information. The commissioner will want to broadcast programmes that earn high audience ratings and reviews:.

Festivals

Festivals attract funders, broadcasters, film-makers and interested parties from around the world who may have many different reasons for attending. Some participants register to see films, some to meet fellow film-makers, some to learn new skills or to join in debates. Some participants want primarily to sell films or ideas, and others to purchase films or ideas, as festivals function extremely effectively as a marketplace. In this marketplace you will get an opportunity to pitch new projects to potential production investors and production partners. There are talks, discussions, viewing opportunities, training sessions and networking events attended by international and national buyers, commissioners, funders and advisors. If you have a film proposal that you want to show to a commissioner, you do not have to wait until the festival to contact them. The delegate list will be published by the festival organisers a few weeks before the festival, and will include contact details of all the participants. It is an acceptable practice to send your proposal to a commissioner to gauge their interest. If the response is positive, a meeting can be arranged to discuss your proposal further. Recommended festivals include:

- American Conservation Film Festival – USA (http://conservationfilm.org)
- Environmental Film Festival – USA (www.dceff.org)
- International Wildlife Film Festival – USA (www.wildlifefilms.org)
- Japan Wildlife Festival – Japan (www.naturechannel.jp)
- Jackson Hole Wildlife Film Festival – USA (www.jhfestival.org)
- Wildscreen Festival – UK (www.wildscreenfestival.org)
- NaturVision Film Festival – Germany (www.natur-vision.de)

There are many other good film festivals, of course, some of which specialise in particular species like birds, or environments such as marine. For a suggested list see www.wildlife-film.com/festivals.html.

Events

Depending on the level of funding you are seeking, it may be worth holding fundraising events to fund your filming project, fully or partly. This can be enjoyable and give you an opportunity to raise awareness of the subject you are planning to film. It also gives the people around you the chance to help you to make the difference you want to make. If you can create a fundraising team of friends, family, colleagues, or activity groups you will make the challenge easier and spread the workload. If you can get interest from your local radio station all the better; it will give you a platform from which to request help, advertise the issues and announce the time and venue of your event.

Agreements between Film-makers and Funders

You will be entering a financial arrangement with the person or people who are responsible for funding your film, so it makes sense to have the arrangement (terms and conditions) really clear for all parties before money changes hands. There are three key areas that should be clarified and included in your agreement:

o   The aims and objectives of each party; exactly what the film (product) being created is; the distribution of the final film; any other outcomes you agree on

o   Who has editorial control of the story; possible input of the funder during production

o   Who has copyright in the film; the agreed budget; the outcomes identified, and how they are to be monitored.

Storytelling

Since early times, people have understood the world and communicated this learning to each other through storytelling. No one has mastered the skill more thoroughly than the Ancient Greeks, long recognised as supreme storytellers. Around 350 BC Aristotle, in his essay called *Poetics*, analysed the structure of successful stories, thus effectively setting out the basis for many modern screenplays. It was Aristotle who documented the insight that a great story needs a beginning (where we meet the characters and discover their situation) a middle (where the story develops, the situation changes and conflict builds) and an end (where the solution is uncovered, the situation resolved – for good or ill, and the main character reaches a point that the audience understand is the end of the matter). These three stages of a story have been translated by film-makers as the three-act structure that is the bedrock of feature films and many one hour-long programmes on television, which are split into three fifteen-to–twenty-minute segments.

There are, of course, other ways to write a story. In the days of the Ancient Greeks, the common belief was that life was guided by all-pervading gods and goddesses, so the Greeks' stories concerned external forces over which the characters had little control, but had to battle against. Other worldviews create other starting points, and in more recent times we are more familiar with stories in which the forces that drive the story forward are internal ones which are played out by the main characters. This approach has been scrutinised and evaluated by many including Joseph Campbell in his book *The Hero with a Thousand Faces*. Here he distilled a lifetime of studying myths, legends and stories from many of the world's cultures into a new comprehension of what constituted the best story-structure: quite simply, a personal journey.

Stories can document real events, people or situations or they can be constructed. Factual stories are often chosen to explore and analyse situations, to enlighten, to be persuasive and indicate different points of view, giving them an authenticity which resonates with the audience. Fictional films can go beyond the boundaries of reality and reveal what is difficult to document, such as internal thought processes: furthermore physical limitations, such as time and location, can be creatively adapted to suit what the writer wants them to say. Both ways of telling a story can be powerful, can entertain, and can reach hearts and minds. But conservation films have an added element: they have an agenda, which is to use storytelling to elicit change.

The Story World

In order to keep the audience engaged, your story world needs to be credible and the 'rules' of that world have to be consistent. There are many ways to do this but here are some basic 'rules' for you to consider:

a) Write about an everyday world the audience is familiar with.

b) All stories need a fundamental premise, a fact about human existence that the audience relates to.

c) A story is created out of the personalities of its characters.

d) Conflict that builds throughout the story keeps the audience interested.

e) Don't short change your audience or insult their intelligence: they need to accept the solution you offer to resolve the story. You can surprise the audience with the unexpected but don't expect them to accept something that would be impossible within your story.

f) Don't offend your audience, especially if you want your film to work on a global scale or in culturally sensitive regions. Certain images, phrases and gestures can be misunderstood by other cultures so do research what is acceptable to your anticipated audience.

Telling Your Story

1. What is the film-making goal – why make the film?

This is probably the most important question you need to ask yourself as you contemplate creating a conservation film. You are about to invest a great deal of time, energy, and possibly money, so be clear about why you are making the film and what it will be about. A good story has the power to inspire and energise – and when people are inspired, they act. Conservation films, conventionally, have at least one of the following intentions:

- to raise awareness
- to promote change
- to give information
- to entertain

49

- to encourage projects
- to communicate a message

2. Who is your audience?

You will be able to match your film to your audience only once you understand who your target audience is going to be. Conservation films, in particular, should be carefully targeted in order to maximise their effectiveness.

a) Consider whether your target audience is a single person (president, company director) a small group (local community, special interest group) or a large group (consumers of international broadcasts and movies).

b) Analyse your target audience, discover what motivates it, examine what it responds to, and decide what will hold its interest for the duration of your film.

c) The research you have completed regarding your audience will indicate what kind of film you need to make, its style and ideal length.

3. Approach

How you decide to tell your story is called the 'approach'; this refers to the various elements of storytelling you choose to use. For example, will you have a narrator tell your story; will you use re-enactments; will you use captions to link your story together; will you use any animation; will your film be shot with natural light or be highly stylised? All these considerations form your 'approach' to your film. Many stories are based on a few very familiar tales, yet they succeed because they bring a new approach or angle to the basic story. The story may have been told before, but you should have your own unique way of retelling it. Your approach, however, will depend on the way your film is being distributed. A film released on social media will need a different approach to a film for broadcast to the world.

4. Styles of documentary

The different traits and conventions used in documentaries were described by the American Bill Nichols:

a) Poetic – a topic that is personal to the people involved (usually the presenter and interviewees), and will emphasise some aspects of those people's lives

b) Participatory – where the events and situation are influenced and altered by the presence of the film-maker.

c) Expository – where an issue is 'exposed', and appeal is made directly to the audience. Such films usually have a narrator emphasising what is happening, as social issues are revealed through a strongly positioned argument.

d) Reflexive – where the audience engages with the content of the documentary as it happens.

e) Observational – a 'fly on the wall' documentary where life is observed in a neutral way without interfering with the subject.

f) Performative – often autobiographical in nature, such films acknowledge the emotional and subjective aspects of documentary film-making.

Film-makers create documentaries in a way that reflects their personality. If they enjoy the planning process then a scripted, in-depth research and storytelling approach will appeal. If this doesn't appeal, then perhaps a 'suck it and see' approach will work, whereby the film-maker follows an unfolding story in a spontaneous way because he or she does do not know exactly how the story will end. Both scripted and non-scripted documentaries can succeed as long as they reach a satisfactory conclusion for the audience.

5. Structure

A story takes the audience on a journey that may last a few minutes or be over two hours long; but whatever the length of your film you will have to keep your audience engaged throughout. The ways to do this are as varied as the number of film-makers, but most films conform to certain rules about the structure:

a) Capture the audience in the opening of the film, give them a reason to continue watching. The first few sequences may be intriguing, heart-rending, amusing or stunningly beautiful, but they will lay the foundations for what is to come.

b) A story needs to be logical; it may not have to follow every event on a day-to-day basis but the audience needs to be able to understand the journey as it unfolds. Your film will be made up of sections or sequences whose number will be in proportion to the length of the film. A short Vine video (six-second videos – see https://vine.co) will have just one sequence, while a feature film can have fifteen or more. The structure of your film is created by putting your sequences in an order that will allow you to manipulate the drama; building it up and then calming it down, then building it up again to reach your conclusion. It is an interesting exercise for new storytellers to see what a difference re-arranging your sequences can make to your story.

c) The unexpected can build drama, anticipation and suspense into your story; cutting from the action to go to another sequence will keep the audience eagerly waiting to return to the first action and find out what happened.

d) In his book *Screenplay* Syd Field examined the idea of important structural points that happen in approximately the same place in most successful films. These are: **Opening Image** – the first image in a film should summarise the entire film, especially its tone. **Exposition** provides some background information to the audience about the plot, characters' histories, setting and theme. **Inciting Incident** is the point at which the main character encounters the problem that will change their life, eg they see an ancient forest demolished to make way for palm oil trees.

6. Creating the story structure

If you are unfamiliar with writing stories for films it is useful, initially, to:

a) Write a short script, say between five and ten minutes long, where you can construct a storyline with a strong narrative structure. This will give you a lot of creative freedom to play with how you engage your audience, introduce your characters, reveal your message and reach your conclusion without it overwhelming you. It is also good practise for those 'teasers' that you will need to create to show to funders and commissioners.

b) Write your story in two or three sentences including the where, what, why, when and who. This exercise will crystallise your story and highlight any gaps that may need further consideration. It is also useful when you are seeking funding to be able to recount in a nutshell what the film is about.

c) Build your sentences into a story outline by considering the three-act structure and writing what will happen in each section. In Act One introduce your character(s), what the issues are, the context of the story, the location. In Act Two develop the story, showing the ups and downs, and what is happening to your characters. In Act Three the final conflict appears, and the resolution is implemented. You will need to check that you have answered any questions you proposed and not leave the audience puzzled or frustrated.

d) This three-act story outline will form the basis of your story or script. If you are creating a documentary then you will probably have some unknown factors at this stage: you may not know what the result of an investigation is, but you do know what you are investigating, whom you can interview, and where this will take place. You are now in a position to write your **shooting script**.

e) The shooting script is an elaboration of the story outline and contains all the detail of the storyline that you want to follow. Here you will write the whole story so you will know exactly what you intend to film. Split your story into short paragraphs that describe the scenes of the story. Think about your structure, where your interviews will come, when you will want to introduce challenge; think about how the audience keeps learning about the key issues, and check if there are any dull or boring sections.

7. Stories: Factual

Factual stories are all around us: we just need to look for them. We walk past them every day, we read about them in the news, we overhear them on public transport, and we discover them in unlikely situations. When you find a story that fascinates, intrigues and excites you, why not discover if other people will have the same reaction? Test it on a few trusted friends, colleagues or even subject experts. If they are genuinely as excited as you are by the story, it is a good indication that it is worth taking it further. It may be useful to follow some of the most popular ways of telling a story to start with:

a) Natural cycles are something we are all familiar with, and our bodies are tuned into, but we experience them mostly on an unconscious level. Opening up our awareness about how nature affects us and other species is a great avenue for film-makers to investigate. Life cycles and dawn-to-dusk stories, for example, provide a framework into which many smaller stories may be woven, which can form a fascinating insight or unique view on a chosen span of time.

b) An expedition to an unfamiliar world could happen on a microscopic level, in a new terrain such as a volcano in a jungle, or even involved a discovery of what is happening in your own back yard. People are naturally inquisitive, and exploring the unknown is fascinating to us.

c) Issue-based films are attractive to conservation film-makers. The challenge is to be able to reveal factual information without alienating the audience by 'preaching'. This can be hard for film-makers who are passionate about their subject and just want to tell the world what is wrong and who is the perpetrator. Ultimately this approach can have the opposite effect to the one intended, if it leaves the audience upset and disempowered. If your story can reveal the issue, show what is at stake, and *offer a solution* the audience will be with you all the way.

d) Projects that have a clearly-defined end goal – such as how to build a rescue centre for wildlife, or returning captive creatures to their original habitat – can inform and entertain your audience at the same time. The audience can identify with the challenge while learning about the people and the wildlife in the process.

e) Conflict is an important story element that your characters should encounter, but the conflict should be one the audience can relate to. Conflict is at the heart of the drama within a story, and human beings love drama. The story should always concentrate upon the central conflict which is revealed, goes through various changes, and finally gets resolved. Smaller side-stories (sub-plots) can be introduced as long as they relate to the central conflict in a way that the audience understands. One example might be the central character having an internal struggle, perhaps the owner of a pristine forest who needs to sell his land to pay for medical bills, and finds the biggest financial offer he receives is from a mining company who will devastate the land, leaving him and his family with a good sum of money but no future and no home. However, there is a different offer from a local NGO with very little money, which would protect the land for future generations and guarantee a home and jobs for the central character – so what should he do, and how might he resolve this conflict? Alternatively, two characters may desire the same thing and will do anything to get their own way; what motivates each character will be revealed as they engage in their battle against each other. The audience will take sides as they decide who is hero and who foe. Both characters should be introduced as early in the story as possible. In some cases the hero is an animal and the foe could be the climatic conditions or the encroachment of humans. In essence, conflict can generate a strong emotional response in your viewers, but they will also need a break from it or they will lose attention. Contrasting conflict with lighter moments (eg humour or affection) can help to balance what can be a roller-coaster ride for the audience.

8. Stories: Fiction

Characters

A constructed story is driven by the personalities of the main characters as they behave according to their own private view of their world. The basic behaviour of the characters should not change during the story until something happens that provides them with new information that may change their belief. The audience that empathises with the character gets to share the emotion and learning of its hero.

a) Characters need to be credible: no one is all good or all bad. Even super-heroes have their flaws, and this is what helps us to relate to them.

b) The audience needs to understand how the characters relate to each other; who is the hero and who is the anti-hero and does this change unexpectedly as the story unfolds? So you have a poacher who changed his or her ways, to become a forest ranger, but who is discovered to have returned to poaching with devastating effect on the animals he or she was supposed to protect?

c) Every story needs just enough characters to tell it, so be careful not to overload your film with unnecessary people.

d) We really have to care about our characters, so there has to be something to care about; even the most flawed character will have redeeming (and possibly unexpected) traits.

e) We want to see characters that we recognise. We don't necessarily have to agree with their motives but we need to understand why, from their perspective, they act as they do.

Time

Time is flexible in the world of films; it is a construct that we can use to help the story by condensing it, making events happen more quickly, or in a different order. You may, of course, decide to run your story through from beginning to end in an entirely linear way, but even here you can add gaps in time to enhance the suspense. Revealing details at the perfect moment engages your audience, making the surprise ending to your film much more rewarding.

Location

Where is your story taking place? The location can create the context for your story, and in the process reveal a lot about your characters. Locations can set the tone or emotion of a story; dark gloomy offices with dense traffic fumes wafting through creates a different expectation from open meadows with dappled sunlight.

9. Writing

As you sit down to research and write your story, then construct your shooting script, strive to make your story both your own and something that other people will want to see. Keep in mind the storytelling information above that will help you to craft your own unique vision into a film that truly resonates with your audience, and ultimately makes a difference.

Conclusion

At the start of this chapter we floated the idea that there are two kinds of forces at play in storytelling, those that originate outside our control, and those that come from within humanity. A conservation film-maker's credo must be, however, to show that this is a false distinction. However much we're tempted to blame 'external' factors – weather, *El Nino* etc for the major changes we're seeing in the natural world, our films must show that man's attitudes and actions are at the root of all this. Unlike Aristotle and his chums we cannot blame the Gods and Goddesses for our plight. To quote William Blake – 'all deities reside within the human breast'.

Production: Gearing Up to Record Images

If you are shooting the film yourself, then before the production phase can start you need to gather together the equipment needed to record images and sound. Choosing the most appropriate camera(s) for the job is an increasingly difficult prospect, as the number and variety of models available is growing all the time. Let's examine the main considerations, to help you make your choice:

Format

We'll start by assuming that you'll be using digital video rather than photographic film. The number of film-makers still using 16mm or 35mm film equipment is dwindling rapidly and the format is likely to die out altogether. The equipment has just become too expensive and heavy, and, being burdened with all the associated problems of requiring rushes to be developed photographically, can't compete with the immediate feedback from video cameras.

Your main format choice with digital video cameras relates to the number of pixels (the smallest controllable elements of a picture represented on the screen), which in turn affects the sharpness of the image. Although there will be other factors such as cost) involved, an important consideration when choosing the format will be how you plan to disseminate your final product. For example, is it for TV broadcast, cinema, the internet, phone apps, DVD release etc?

The main digital video formats available can be summarised as follows:

SD – Standard Definition – the screen ratio (for PAL systems) is 720 x 576 pixels (width x height). This is the size of a classic widescreen television based on a cathode ray tube (CRT) – large and heavy, not manufactured any more and gradually being superseded, although quite a few homes still use them. This is also the format of DVDs. Note that the number of horizontal lines generating the picture is different in the UK and many other countries (PAL: 576 lines) and the USA and parts of South America (NTSC: 486 lines).

HD – High Definition – there are various options in terms of the numbers of pixels, the most common formats being 1280 x 720 (sometimes called HD Ready when specified in association with television sets) and 1920 x 1080 (often referred to as Full High Definition). Most flat-screen televisions available these days are Full and this is also the format for Blu-Ray Discs (BD). To watch programmes in high definition the user needs not only to have an HD TV set but also to be able to receive HD transmissions. This could be via a BD player (although these have not become as popular with the public as the manufacturers initially hoped), or via Freeview, Freesat or a cable or satellite television supplier. The main television broadcasters have HD channels, but many of the smaller ones still use SD.

UHD – Ultra High Definition – again there is an increasing number of options available, the most common being 4K. This corresponds to pixel counts of 3840 x 2160 or 4096 x 2160. You can buy 4K television sets, though at the time of writing there are few broadcasts in 4K. This format is certain to become more popular, however, and 4K cameras are coming down in price all the time. This format is also being used for cinema (movie theatre) productions and it doesn't stop there – 6K and 8K cameras are in production for Super High Vision, although these are very expensive and aimed largely at the cinema producer. Cameras like these are rapidly replacing 35mm film for cinema, but are also being used for some television productions. Be aware that shooting in 4K will produce large file sizes. Some camera operators shoot 4K, but downsize to 1080 in the edit; this creates superb quality.

The question we are asked more than any other is which cameras are 'broadcast quality' (commonly referred to as 'broadcast-safe' or 'broadcast-legal' in the industry). Increasingly broadcasters will now accept films only in HD, so if you're aiming to produce films for television you really need to focus on HD or 4K. But not any old HD camera will do – many broadcasters adhere strictly to the technical or regulatory broadcast requirements of the target area or region the feed might be broadcasting to. In most of Europe the standards are set by the European Broadcasting Union (EBU) – you can download their latest guides via www.ebu.ch. In the United States the regulatory body is the Federal Communications Commission (FCC) and their website is www.fcc.gov. Here you will be able to compare the technical requirements with the specifications of various cameras, but in practice it may be more productive simply to talk to camera operators or producers who supply certain broadcasters, to find out what the favourite platforms currently are.

High-end kit used for television is often still beyond the budget of the newcomer, however. As well as frequently being asked whether a camera is 'broadcast quality', we are increasingly coming across aspiring film-makers who are saving up for the ultimate camera that will fulfil all their needs including possible future television broadcast. This is a dangerous path to follow! If you're starting out now, the chances are that by the time you've made a film worthy of broadcast, technical requirements will have changed, and your dream camera will no longer be up to the job. Not only that, but if you make a programme for television in future it is quite likely that the camera used will be hired in for the job, or lent to you by the producers. So don't worry about owning the perfect camera to start with.

So far we've mainly been talking about cameras for television, but if your film's destination is the internet, DVD or phone apps, then more affordable HD options will be fine (such as those found on many DSLR (Digital Single Lens Reflex) cameras these days, or on HD handycam-style camcorders). SD cameras, such as those recording on to miniDV tapes, can also be used but they are rapidly being superseded by budget HD versions.

Sensors

When light enters the lens of your camera it is focused on to a sensor (or a number of sensors) that has an array of thousands, or millions, of tiny cells that convert the light into electrons. This electrical current is converted into digital information that can then be stored on solid state memory,  disc, tape or whatever recording medium the camera uses. The two most common types of sensor are CCD (charge-coupled device) and CMOS (complementary metal-oxide semiconductor).

Camcorders use one or three CCDs – those with three are designed to record red, green and blue colours separately, which produces a superior image. They are gradually being replaced by systems with one CMOS sensor, however, as these use less power and can capture images at higher speeds.

Sensors also come in a variety of sizes, often measured in inches (across the diagonal) such as 1/5in, 1/4in, 1/3in, 1/2in, or referred to in other ways such as APS-C (23.6 x 15.8mm is commonly referred to as Super 35 or S35 in the camcorder world) or Full Frame (36 x 24mm). In very general terms the larger the sensor, the better quality the picture. Larger sensor cameras are usually more expensive and will allow you to shoot with a shallower depth of field (which may or may not be what you want).

One other factor to bear in mind is that a smaller sensor will increase the effective focal length of a mounted lens. This is often referred to as the crop-factor, and may be an issue if you wish to shoot images that are far away (often the case with wildlife!). A camera with a smaller sensor and a budget telephoto lens may allow you more highly magnified images than if you were using a more expensive camera with a larger sensor.

Bitrate

This term refers to the speed with which footage is recorded to memory (ie to the number of bits, or units of information, processed per unit of time. With digital video we are normally measuring in Mbit/s (Mega (million) bits per second). The higher the bitrate, the higher the quality of the recorded image.

When you are comparing cameras it is important to check bitrates, especially if you are filming for television, because many broadcasters have a minimum bitrate that they will accept (and this is routinely increasing at present). Acceptable criteria are again regulated by EBU and FCC. The bitrate speed is governed by the recording part of your camera, so if you need to increase your bitrate it is possible, with some cameras, to add on a faster recording unit, rather than replacing the entire camera. For example, if your camera records on to its own media at 36 Mbit/s, and the BBC requires a minimum of 50 Mbit/s, you may be able to record directly on to a separate drive at 200 Mbit/s and get round the problem. It tends to be only the higher end cameras, however, that allow you to add on external drives in the first place.

Optical Zoom Size

If your camera has a fixed lens then the size of the optical zoom will be important. The optical zoom capability is often expressed as a magnification factor: x10, x15 etc. Don't get this confused with 'digital' zoom, which is an electronic magnification of the image already captured, and which can lead to pixelated or blocky images. If you see a camera offering x600 zoom for example, this will be digital zoom and can safely be ignored as its use effectively reduces the pixel density of the image. When setting up a digital camcorder you can, in many models, actually switch off the digital zoom so that it's not used accidentally (by default some cameras switch over seamlessly to digital zoom when their optical zoom limit is reached).

You might find a x10 zoom limiting if you are wanting to film subjects far away, so you would get better results from a camera with a larger optical zoom or with interchangeable lenses (see below). For many cameras with fixed lenses you can get wide-angle or telephoto attachments that fit on to the end of the lens. For example you can get 2x or 3x teleconverters for many camcorders, which simply double or triple the magnification of the image. Cheap attachments can lead to poor quality images though, so do check reviews or try before you buy.

Interchangeable Lenses

If a camera can take different lenses, then this opens up lots of other possibilities. As well as your general zoom or telephoto lens you will be able to buy wide-angle lenses for scenic shots or use in enclosed places, macro lenses for close-ups, and so on. Lenses can be very expensive – in some cases more expensive than the camera – so do research options carefully before you buy. If you needed a specific lens only for one particular sequence in your film it might be better to borrow or hire it, or team up with another camera operator who has the right kit.

Many camcorders can take a variety of lenses with the right adaptors. So if you have a number of Canon, Nikon, Sigma or Tamron lenses for your stills camera, for example, you can use these on some camcorders with the appropriate adaptor. As mentioned when we discussed sensors, there may be a magnification factor involved. As these lenses were designed for 35mm film, when used on  your camcorder the sensor only collects light from part of the centre of the image – 1/3inch for example. The result is a higher magnification than you would expect (7.2x higher in this case, so a 100–300 zoom would give you the equivalent magnification of a 720–2,160 zoom on your SLR camera!). This is a great bonus when filming close-ups at a distance – but remember the higher the magnification the more stable the camcorder set-up needs to be, to prevent image-wobble.

When you are choosing lenses the main numbers to watch out for are the focal length (in mm) and the aperture (f number). The higher the focal length, the greater the magnification. A lens with a focal length less than 50mm may be considered wide-angle, and above 50mm to be telephoto. Prime lenses have a fixed focal length; they are often of high quality, but can be expensive, and of course will need changing every time you want a different perspective. Zoom lenses will cover a range: for example, a 12--24mm zoom would make a very useful wide-angle lens; a 100--300mm zoom would be a good telephoto for shooting subjects further away and for close ups. A good starting kit would include at least a wide-angle and a telephoto zoom to cover the most common eventualities.

The f number signifies the maximum aperture of a lens; the smaller the number, the larger the aperture. An f2.8 lens will let in more light than an f4 lens, and so will allow you to shoot in low light conditions without getting camera shake. Lenses with low f numbers tend to be more expensive than those with higher, due to the optical quality of the lens elements. Zoom lenses may have a range of f numbers because, as you zoom in, the maximum aperture available reduces.

More and more lenses produced these days are cine-style. These have 'de-clicked', smooth iris rings, so that the visible light change is continuous, not in steps, as you open or close the iris. Also, cine lenses are totally manual and have gears/teeth on the outside to mesh with follow-focus systems. Cine lenses usually have a 300° focus throw, which means focus is very precise, but takes lots of turns to get from close-up to infinity.

Extra Sockets

Budget cameras tend to have few sockets for you to plug in devices such as microphones and headphones. This may not be an issue depending on how you will be recording your sound (we discuss this in a later chapter). If you are using your camera to record sound as well as vision, then it is recommended that you at least have a  headphone socket so that you can monitor the recorded sound, and ideally a stereo 3.5mm jack socket or XLR sockets for plugging in better microphones. XLR (Cannon **X** connector, **L**ocking, **R**esilient) sockets are larger, and considered more professional as they allow you to use 'balanced' cables – these cancel out radio- interference, so long cables don't act as radio-aerials – as well as higher quality microphones.

Ease of Use

This may sound counter-intuitive, but some of the budget cameras, which appear to have few controls, can actually be harder to use in the field. This is because their controls are buried within menus that can be fiddly to access, whereas on larger cameras the controls are often clearly-located and can be accessed and operated swiftly.

Even basic operations like zoom and focus can be much harder and more time-consuming to use via a menu system, rather than simply by rotating rings on the lens itself, which can be reached instantly. Furthermore, changing focus by pushing on a touch-screen is not the best option: the pressure required can wobble the camera slightly.

Frame Rate

This is a measure of how quickly frames (single images) can be recorded by the camera system. The most commonly-used rates are 25fps (frames per second) in Europe and 24fps in the US, but there are many other possibilities. When images are played back at these rates the movement appears fluid and flickerless – the basic aspiration of all movie cameras.

With digital cameras you often find the frame rate and recording system referred to as either 'p' or 'i', as in 25p or 50i, for example. The letters refer to *progressive* (when frames are recorded and played back one after the other, as is the case with photographic movie cameras) or *interlaced* (when each frame is recorded twice, with alternate lines recorded each time). There are some cameras where you can switch between the two, but most will use either the progressive or the interlaced system. There are differences in the results, and to a certain extent these are subjective. The progressive system is often thought of as being more 'film-like', whereas the interlaced system is more clinical and sharp. You will especially notice differences when there is movement in the frame or you are panning. 25p is often described as being 'choppy', especially when a pan is performed too quickly. A lot of Panasonic cameras don't give the option of 25p – only 50p, as the standard speed. Playing back from their cameras, on a 25p timeline, the result looks just like 25P; but it offers the option of changing the speed, to give a slowmo effect.

63

Some cameras, especially the higher-end ones, can offer higher frame rates, such as 100fps or 200fps. This will enable you to record at a higher speed so that, in playback, motion appears slowed down (slowmo). This is an increasingly popular technique, especially with wildlife: in fact there are some wildlife movies made for cinema where the entire film has been played back at 95% normal speed to add that slightly dreamier quality. Even the iPhone 6 records at 240fps in 1080 HD (clips shot in this way have even made it into a high end BBC NHU programmes!).

But for super-slow motion shots (such as water drops splashing or butterflies flapping their wings slowly) you will need to use super-high-speed digital cameras such as the Photron, Phantom or i-SPEED models. These can record (up to) tens of thousands of frames per second, enough to slow down the fastest humming bird's wing-beat, or chameleon's darting tongue, dramatically.

But these are expensive pieces of kit – some costing over £100,000 per camera – so they are likely to be hired in for the sequence rather than owned by the film-maker. The operation of equipment like this is a specialist skill, and it is probable you would hire an operator along with the kit for a day or two as required.

Recording Media

Another aspect of camera technology that has recently changed rapidly is the media used for storing the footage. Initially all video cameras used tape (first analogue, then digital) and some still do. But then hard drives came on the scene, and increasingly cameras are now using solid-state technology: recording on to memory cards/chips. This has huge advantages for the conservation film-maker – many hours of HD footage and sound can be recorded on to small, relatively inexpensive, cards, easily carried in the field, which can be downloaded to a hard drive much faster than real-time. They are also easily concealed if you are worried about your footage being confiscated.

Note that memory cards record at different speeds. The speed, often referred to as the class – is shown as a number up to 10 in the letter 'C' on the label. If you are buying cards for a digital film camera, make sure you buy the fastest you can – class 10 recommended – to avoid dropouts.

This brings us to a crucial new area of film technology – that of handling data. It's essential to understand all the various means of storage, transfer, bitrates, file-types and the all-important matter of backing-up important material. Larger production teams may have someone with a thorough grounding in these developing digital technologies to handle this side of things. This role is known by some as DIT (Digital Imaging Technician); though the tasks are often performed by an assistant or by the camera operator.

Applications

The situation in which you're recording may well influence which camera is right for the job. If you want to avoid looking like a professional film-maker – to film undercover in a bush-meat market for example – then a DSLR that can shoot video may well be your best bet. You can pretend you're just taking tourist snaps while actually you're filming illegal activities. Another approach is to use a small camera concealed in a bag or your clothing, its lens peeping through a discreet hole, or even using a mobile phone's video camera.

DSLR cameras are increasingly being used for film-making, as many models can shoot HD video, with a shallow depth of field that many favour. With their large sensors, the quality of the picture can be superb. There are practical downsides, such as the difficulty in creating smooth zooms, but there is an ever-growing number of fixes and add-on gadgets to help. DSLR cameras come in a vast range of models and prices, but even some of the mid-range lower-budget ones can shoot HD video.

Conversely you may be working for a larger production company or broadcaster where you need to be seen to be a professional camera operator – in which case a higher-end video camera and sturdy tripod will be minimum requirements.

We are also seeing an array of more specialist, but very affordable, cameras of great use to the conservation film-maker. Some of these can be very small, such as action-cams (for example the GoPro series). These were initially designed as sports cameras – to be strapped to a cyclist's helmet, or the front of a racing kayak – but they have many other applications: for instance they can be attached to a pole and used underwater (since many come with their own waterproof housing) and, thanks to their rugged build, put in many hazardous situations where you wouldn't want to risk your main camera. They can record in high quality HD, up to 4K, to a memory card; and with their small size they are also useful in situations where you need to conceal your film-making. Of course this wouldn't be your only camera – you can't change lenses or focus on many models, as they are just point-and-shoot – but they can help you get unusual footage to make your film stand out.

Cost

For many, of course, this will be the main consideration! Alongside the development of professional cameras we have seen advances in budget cameras aimed at the amateur or semi-pro market. This has really opened up possibilities for the newcomer, who can now create quality films on a tiny budget. Although the bitrate and other aspects may not be enough to please a broadcaster, budget gear can enable a film-maker to produce excellent material for use on DVD/BD or for the internet or other applications. It is easier and cheaper than ever to make films now – you can buy a small HD camera and a laptop with an editing program for just a few hundred pounds/dollars, and do it all yourself. The process of actually making a complete film will teach you a great deal, and it is more affordable than ever.

If your film is to be broadcast on television then it is important to find out in advance whether the broadcaster has any stipulations regarding equipment to be used, including bitrates etc. They may insist on a 4K production even if is to be initially broadcast in HD and SD. It may well be the case that you have to hire in specialist camera(s) to suit an individual production. Also find out if there is a percentage of the film that can be shot at lower resolutions. For example there may be cases where a broadcaster will allow an HD production to include 10% shot in SD, which will open it up to allow the use of other cameras or older non-HD stock footage for a small proportion of the final movie.

Whatever your main camera is, it's a good idea to have a backup, especially when travelling in the field or abroad, where it may be difficult to replace or repair a camera if anything goes wrong or equipment is stolen or confiscated. If your main camera is a dedicated video camcorder, then a DSLR that shoots video will be a good backup, and can also be used for taking stills throughout the production and for time-lapse sequences (as discussed in the next chapter).

If you are on a budget and a DSLR is your main camera, then an HD handycam-style camcorder is a good bet for a backup. These are small, lightweight, record on to SD cards, often have a good optical zoom, and produce surprisingly good images for the low cost.

As you can see, there is a huge amount to consider when choosing camera equipment. The main thing is to get started and to practise with what you've got, accepting that you are likely to be upgrading many times in your career as budgets, specifications and demands change. Don't forget that with a conservation film, the message and content is the most important aspect; so, depending on where it is to be broadcast, a small action-cam, or even a phone's camera, may get you the footage you need.

If you're overwhelmed by the choices available we recommend going on a short course where you can try a range of cameras and talk to professionals who use them in the field (such as Wildeye's Wildlife Camera Operator Course: www.wildeye.co.uk/wildlife-camera-operator).

Other Useful Equipment

Support

In most cases it's essential to support your camera as much as possible for steady, professional-looking shots. A tripod is the best accessory for this, as it also allows you smooth camera movements. When choosing a tripod think about its weight: a heavy tripod will certainly be steadier, but can you carry it long distances and easily take it where your camera goes (on an aircraft for example)?

One of the most important factors when selecting a

67

tripod, however, is how smoothly the head moves when you pan (move from side to side) and tilt (move up and down) – fluid-heads are the best, and of course the most expensive. So try out tripods– preferably with your own camera – in a shop before you buy: pan and tilt and check for any jarring or vibration. Like cameras, tripods come in a huge range of sizes, types and prices.

Note that the size of the tripod will be dictated to some degree by the size of your camera. A larger camcorder will need a heavier, sturdier tripod, while a DSLR will manage on a smaller one. Large tripods tend to be heavier and more costly, with better fluid-heads, whereas smaller ones are easier to pack and carry in the field. One of the main disadvantages with light-weight tripods is they can vibrate if conditions are windy.

There will be situations where using a tripod is inappropriate – when you are trying to look like a tourist, working undercover, for example, or moving around a lot, in a busy market. On such occasions always look for other ways to stabilise the camera unobtrusively; even leaning on a tree or building while you're filming can make a huge difference.

Here a medium weight tripod is used to support a camcorder while filming termite mounds in Tanzania

Monopods can also be used, for example in vehicles where there is no room to set up a tripod. If you do a lot of work from a vehicle you may find a clamp system useful. It's basically the head of a tripod attached to a clamp that you can fasten to the bars or window ledge of the vehicle to keep your camera steady.

Film-makers are increasingly keen to incorporate shots where the camera itself is moving during the shot. As well as panning and tilting on a tripod this can be achieved using cranes, jibs and tracks that enable you to swing or push the camera smoothly in all directions. Although they can be cumbersome to carry and use in the field, if you have a small camcorder or DSLR there are various portable and foldable models available which have become really quite affordable. These will add a further dimension to the shots you can achieve, especially in situations where you can plan ahead. Unless you have a remote monitor, you won't be able to see the image the camera is recording, so there'll be a lot of trial and error, especially when you start out with a new jib system.

A clamp with a tripod head used to steady a camcorder on the roof of a Land Rover while filming lions in Kenya

A beanbag is a really useful addition to your kit. It will steady your camera in many awkward situations – on a rock, the car window ledge, on a boat, on grass etc. You can buy them ready-made or make your own using a soft waterproof material of a suitable size to support your camera. Fill the bag with something like rice that will not be too noisy as it moves around; do not overfill. You may need to experiment for a while until you get the right size and shape of beanbag but it's well worth the effort. If you are travelling abroad you can take the beanbag empty (to save on weight and volume) and fill with beans/sand etc when you arrive on location.

Having said all of that, there are some conservation film-makers, such as Richard Brock (brockinitiative.org), who have shot all the footage for many successful films entirely handheld!

Using a beanbag on a fence to steady a camcorder

Lights

You are most likely to want to use lights if you are filming indoors or in a dark outdoor enclosed situation, such as inside an animal burrow. Lighting for filming has taken leaps forward in the last few years with the development of LED arrays. These can be purchased in a number of sizes with different numbers of LEDs – and therefore brightness. They have many advantages

70

over traditional film lights: they are smaller, cheaper, run on batteries and produce a cool light (essential when filming creatures, in macro, that can be affected by heat, especially insects and amphibians). Place these lights on the ground or a support, rather than handholding them, so the shadows don't wobble around.

If you are working on a set you are better off with a couple of lights, so you can move them around to eliminate shadows and create the lighting effect you want. Don't always go for the obvious front-lit, few-shadows option – sometimes a subject lit from the side or back can produce a more dramatic shot. As in so many aspects of film-making with video, the best way to learn is to experiment with different techniques, view your footage on a television, and make notes about which results you prefer.

Shooting in the Dark

If you need to film in the dark – nocturnal animals or illegal night-time activities for example – you have three main options:

Image intensifier or starlight cameras – these are specialist bits of kit that are very expensive, and are typically hired in for a specific shoot. They work by massively increasing what available light there is, so they will not work in complete darkness.

Thermal cameras are also expensive, and are used to film anything that gives off heat, such as animals. The images appear as bright-coloured shapes, representing the heat emitted by the subject, so tend to be used only in small portions of a film.

Infra-red (IR) is by far the most common technique for filming in the dark. For this you need a camera that can record infra-red images (which many camcorders do, including some of the budget handycams) and a source of IR light. This technique can be used in complete darkness and results in a monochrome image, often with a greenish tint. Camcorders which can record infra-red have a small number of IR-emitting LEDs around the lens, but these often have a range of only a few metres. To film anything further away you can use the same camera, but will need larger IR-emitting lights. You can buy dedicated units for this, or make your own using car headlights, covered with IR film, and connected to a car battery. These can be shone in the direction the camera is filming, and will illuminate subjects at far greater distances.

IR also has the benefit that most animals cannot see the light and will continue behaving normally, which would probably not be the case if they were spotlit with conventional lighting.

Power

At the very least have two batteries for you camera – so one can be recharging while you use the other. If you will be in the field for long periods without access to a charger you will need several high-capacity batteries. Other bits of kit, such as connectors that allow you to recharge your batteries from a car battery, or small solar panel chargers, can be very useful.

You can buy batteries of different capacities – the one on the right, which came with the camera, will last about 45 minutes in the field; the one on the left gives you about 3 hours – much more suitable for situations where you may be far from a charge

Filming Techniques

Once you are familiar with the basic controls of your chosen camera, it's time to practise some common and useful filming techniques:

Handling the camera

The most basic shots, when the camera is on a tripod and not moving at all, are called *locked-off* shots. Remember that when you press the record button – when you start and stop filming – it will jog the camera; so always wait a few seconds at the end of a shot before pressing the button, to give enough room to end the shot nicely in the edit (you may want a fade-out, for example).

Also be aware that camera-shake or -movement will be greatly magnified as you zoom in on a subject. If possible, therefore, move closer to the subject rather than zooming in. If you are using a long telephoto lens even the tiniest vibration can ruin a shot: a sturdy tripod or other support will be essential.

If you can't use any support and are holding the camera while recording, you need to steady your elbows: keep them pulled in to your body, or kneel on one knee and rest your elbow on the other.

Viewfinders and Screens

Many camcorders these days give you the option of using either the viewfinder (some of which produce an image in colour, some in black and white) or a flip-out mini LCD screen in colour. Some DSLRs and smaller camcorders have only a screen – ideally you should be able to rotate this to a position to suit the situation.

Some camera operators, if they're accustomed to using the viewfinders of film cameras, prefer to use them on video camcorders too; but you should use whichever you feel most comfortable with, and whichever you find easiest to focus with. In bright conditions you may find it hard to see the LCD screen, so revert to the viewfinder if your camera has one. Note that if you use an LCD screen in bright light, your images may be overexposed. The pupils of your eyes will have contracted to combat the brightness, and therefore the image on your screen will look misleadingly darker. Your initial reaction will be to increase the exposure of your image so it looks right in the bright light. The opposite is true in darker conditions. (Some prosumer and professional cameras have a feature (often called 'zebra pattern') that you can set to show you which parts of the image are well exposed).

Focus

In general if you are filming animals or people it is best to focus on the eye of the main subject (this is true with still photography too). This is especially important with close-ups and macro work, where you may be so close that only part of the subject can be in focus (shallow depth of field discussed below).

It is recommended that you practise using manual focus as much as possible. If your subject moves off shot while you are filming it in automatic focus mode (autofocus), your camera will refocus the lens on whatever lies behind. If the subject then comes back into shot it will be out of focus for a while, and you'll see the camera 'hunt' for focus, thereby ruining the shot. There are many other situations where automatic focus can spoil a take – so use it sparingly, if at all. If you have to film through the bars of a cage in a zoo or pet-market, stand close and focus manually on the subject, to prevent the camera autofocusing on the wire.

Some cameras have a push-button autofocus; this enables you to autofocus quickly on a subject, by briefly pushing the button, and the camera/lens essentially stays in manual focus mode afterwards. This can be very useful if you don't trust the accuracy of your focusing, or if bright sunlight makes it difficult for you to see the LCD screen well enough.

Throwing focus can be an effective technique if you don't overuse it. It involves shifting the concentration of the viewer from one subject to another using focus – for example we may start a shot focused on a rhino peacefully grazing and then *throw* focus to the ranger in the background, providing protection from poachers.

Pulling focus is the opposite – refocusing on a subject closer to the camera. Of course you need to use manual focus for this, and practise the technique.

Depth of Field

Depth of field is the amount of the image that is also in focus, in front of and behind the subject. If your subject is in focus, and all the environment around it is also sharp, you may describe that shot as having a wide depth of field – or deep focus. This is fine in many situations. But if only a small part of the image is in focus – let's say a close-up on the head of a gecko produces a shot with the eye in focus, but the tip of the snout and anything from the neck backwards out of focus – then you would describe this shot as having a narrow depth of field, or shallow focus.

The factors determining the depth of field are:

- Distance from camera to subject – the greater the distance, the greater the depth of field.

- The focal length of the lens (or the amount you are zoomed in). At the telephoto end you'll have a narrower depth of field than with a wide-angle setting. This is also why, when following movement (an animal receding into the distance, for example), the wider the setting the less likely the subject is to go out of focus.

- Aperture size – a narrow iris (high f number) in bright conditions will produce a greater depth of field.

You can manipulate these three factors to create the depth of field you require. For example, portraits of animals -- such as the head of a cheetah against a busy bush-background -- may look more attractive if the background is out of focus, causing the subject's head to stand out more. You could achieve this by zooming in on the head and/or moving closer or by opening the iris wider (see below).

Exposure

This refers to the amount of light admitted into the camera by the iris. The iris is an opening between the lens and the sensor which narrows to reduce the entry of light when conditions are very bright and vice versa. Some users leave their cameras on automatic exposure, which can produce perfect exposure in static situations, but it pays to experiment with the manual options, as slight changes in the background lighting will cause the exposure to shift.

Some cameras have a backlight compensation button which, when pressed, opens the iris a little to allow more light through. You would use this when shooting a subject against a bright background – filming a bird in a tree, against a bright sky, is a classic example. Using only autoexposure, the bird would appear very dark, as the camera adjusts exposure for the bright sky; so use the backlight button to increase the incoming light and brighten the bird (or use manual exposure, of course). Either way, the sky may appear very white: but as the bird is the subject of interest, you have to live with that.

75

Another situation where you would need manual exposure is when you are panning from a dark area to a bright area, or *vice versa*. Let's say you were filming a bird perched in a tree, which then took off and flew into a bright sky. In automatic mode you would see the subject suddenly darken as the background became brighter, which might well ruin the shot – manual exposure mode will prevent this.

Shutter Speed

In cameras that use chemical film, this is the amount of time the shutter is open, allowing light to fall on a single frame of the film. In digital video cameras, it is the amount of time an electrical charge is supplied to the sensor to enable it to record a single frame. A high shutter speed freezes motion (as it would in a stills photograph) to produce a blur-free shot. A slower shutter speed may be useful for 'creative' shots, such as blurred motion during a fast-action sequence.

The rule of thumb is the shutter speed should be half the frame rate. So, if you are shooting at 25 frames per second (fps), then set the shutter to 1/50th. If you let the camera select shutter speed automatically then sometimes it will give you a very high speed and make the shot have a staccato effect that looks very unnatural.

White balance

This is the adjustment of the intensities of colours to ensure that specific ones (particularly neutrals and white) are displayed correctly. You may see some camera operators holding a piece of white card in front of their camera before recording. This is to show the camera what 'true white' is in the current lighting situation so it can set the correct white balance. Your camera is likely to have this facility – check the manual and try experimenting before you get in the field.

Light entering your camera will have different hues depending on its source. The light temperature is measured in Kelvin (K):

- Tungsten bulbs indoors produce a warm yellow light (3,000K)
- Fluorescent tubes/bulbs and many low-energy bulbs produce a white light (5,000K)
- Natural light on a cloudy day produces bright white light (6,500K)
- Natural light on a bright, cloudless day produces a pale-blue light (sometimes over 10,000K, depending on where the lens is pointing)

4,300K is a good manual setting for mixed light. Although your camera can automatically try to correct the white balance it is best to adjust this manually.

Otherwise, if you were filming a sunset for example, the camera might adjust the balance as if it were indoors – creating an image with boosted blues and not letting you capture the rich oranges and reds you desire. So, experiment with your camera's white balance settings in these situations.

Composition

For some, setting up a good-looking shot in the frame comes naturally, for others it is a skill that can be learnt and practised. There are a few helpful rules that you can bear in mind when composing your pictures:

- **The Rule of Thirds** – this technique involves imagining that your frame is divided into three, vertically and horizontally, giving you four points where the lines cross. These are known as the *thirds*. Avoid the tendency to place your subject in the centre of the frame – it almost always looks more aesthetically pleasing when placed on one of the thirds.

Note the shot has been composed with the head of the lioness on the top left third – a more pleasing effect than having it in the centre

Similarly a landscape looks better if the horizon is on one of the horizontal thirds rather than half way down the frame. Which third you use depends on the situation, and which part of the picture is of most interest. If you are filming a sunset, for example, it is likely that the sky and the clouds are of most interest, so the horizon should be on the lower third. Again, this technique is just as applicable when shooting stills.

- **Looking-room** – if your subject is looking to one side, make sure you frame it so it has plenty of space to look, into as in the example above.

- **Walking-room** – similarly if your subject is moving towards one side of the frame, and you are panning/tracking to follow this, make sure you leave it plenty of room to move into. If the tail end of the animal goes out of frame now and again this doesn't matter – but if the head goes out of frame it will ruin the shot.

In this shot of a lion cub in the Masai Mara in Kenya at sunset, the composition places the horizon in the lower third, as the more interesting area is the clouds behind the cub rather than the ground below it.

Shot size

Don't fall into the trap of using just mid-shots where the whole subject is in frame; combine these with a few wide shots (also known as *establishing* shots) to give a sense of scale and location, and some extreme close-ups – focusing on the eye or hand for example.

In any situation always aim to get at least three basic shots – a wide, a mid and a close-up – before trying others. Aim for maybe just ten seconds of each shot. Then even if the situation changes (such as the subject bird flying away) after just thirty seconds, you still have three shots that can be edited together to make a mini-sequence. Once you have those three basic shots in the bag then you can consider others, maybe changing angle or position, thinking more creatively.

Wide

Mid

Close-up

Shooting sequences

Always keep in mind that, while editing, you will be building your shots into a series of sequences that tell a story. So get a variety of shots that will cut together well. If you come across an interesting or dynamic situation, the instinctive tendency is to keep recording in case you miss something – but doing that can leave you with hours of similar shots that are difficult to edit together.

When you watch documentaries on television you will see that the vast majority of shots are less than ten seconds long – many of them only fractions of a second (especially where there is fast action on screen). So compose your shot (let's say you start with a mid-shot), record about ten seconds, stop recording, recompose a close-up, record another ten seconds or so, stop, pull back to record the wide, and so on. You will find these shots much easier to edit together and it will force you to think about composition and sequences. And of course always be prepared to break rules – if you are following some *really* important action keep following it. You can always compose some wide shots later.

Shooting ratio

The amount of footage you record compared to the amount used in your finished film is known as the *shooting ratio*. For example if you recorded ten hours of raw footage (often called *rushes*), and then edited this down to a thirty-minute movie, your shooting ratio would be 20:1.

In the days when film stock was an expensive part of the budget, the shooting ratio was very important and camera operators were encouraged to work towards a low ratio. Now that you can buy relatively cheap memory cards that can hold hours of footage you may think this is no longer an issue – but if you shoot thirty hours of footage (a high shooting ratio of 60:1 if you are making a thirty-minute movie) you will find reviewing the rushes and then editing the final movie a much larger task. If you were paying an editor/studio per hour, then this would significantly affect the budget. But even working on your own production you will find it harder in the edit stage if you have a high shooting ratio.

So think about how important each shot is, and where it will fit in the story, before you hit the record button. Also think about the composition and length of each shot in advance of recording. If something goes wrong then by all means repeat shots, and if something unusual or exciting is happening then of course keep rolling to catch all the action. But planning each shot (whether mentally on-the-spot, or on paper in advance) usually results in better footage and a lower shooting ratio.

Zooming

Shots including a zoom action are often left out in the edit unless you are emphasising a distance or zooming as a particular effect. It can be effective to focus on the head of your subject for example and then zoom out to show how far away it is, or to reveal its location. It works the other way around too – zooming in on a distant tree to reveal the small creature hiding in the leaves and so on (but do this very sparingly). Of course use the zoom to compose your shot, but don't record endless zooms unless they are important creatively. Too many zooms in a movie are quickly tiring and distracting to the watcher; they are disparagingly known as *tromboning*!

A rapid zoom in an action sequence – often known as a *crash zoom* – can be impressive. For example, if you were filming a wide shot of a lion chasing a zebra, you could then crash zoom into a close up of the lion's head as the death-grip is made to the zebra's throat and the chase comes to a stop.

The zoom can also help with your focusing: if you are about to record a wide shot and are not sure if the main subject is sharp, then zoom in first, check focus in manual, then zoom back to the wide before hitting the record button.

81

Camera Angles

If you are filming animals then get down to the level of the creatures you are recording, especially with small animals such as insects. Put the camera right down on the ground if necessary – mini LCD monitors that you can swivel up are useful in this situation. Looking up at something is nearly always more interesting than looking down, but often the best approach is to get the lens at the same level as the eye of the subject – known as the *eyeline*.

The tendency when using tripods is to set them up at a comfortable standing height, but this is often not the best nor most creative height for the subject you are filming. So when you are setting up a tripod always think about the height before you lock the camera on top.

Panning

This technique can be used to survey the scene you are recording, or to follow the movement of an animal, person or vehicle. Note the classic technique of following an animal for a certain distance, or while it displays a certain behaviour, and then stopping the pan to let the animal walk out of frame – this produces an excellent cut-point or sequence end. The corollary being starting the camera rolling on an empty spot and letting the creature move into the shot before following it with a pan movement.

Panning can also be used to move the viewer's attention from one subject to another. For example you could be filming a group of lions feeding on a kill, and then pan to one side to reveal the hyenas waiting for the lions to move off the carcass.

If you are panning to show a landscape always practise the pan several times before pressing the record button: get the speed right and the start and finish points where you want them. When you are ready, start recording, count a few seconds, then start the pan; pan smoothly to the finish point then count another few seconds before stopping recording – this gives you plenty of scope in the edit to use the pan in different ways.

The speed of a pan will depend on the situation, the effect you want, and the distance you are panning. But keep in mind that an average pan lasts about ten seconds. If in retrospect it seems a little too slow it can be speeded up slightly in the edit.

**Preparing a landscape pan – in this case using a camcorder
on a tripod to pan across the rainforest in Ecuador
from the summit of Armadillo Mountain**

Tilting

This technique (sometimes called a vertical pan) has similar rules to panning but involves tilting the camera up or down. For example shots starting at the base of a tree and tilting up into the canopy can be very effective. Again – always practise first, keep the movement smooth, and use a tripod if at all possible.

Tracking

This technique involves following a subject or action by moving the camera rather than just panning from one fixed position. Practise moving on foot with the camera – in particular you want to avoid the camera bobbing up and down as you walk. Larger productions where the shots can be pre-planned may use tracks (similar to railway tracks) and dollies (wheeled contraptions that hold the camera steady and run on the rails) but these are expensive, heavy and difficult to use in the field or rough terrain.

Steadicams involve a harness with weights worn by the camera operator, enabling him or her to keep the camera relatively steady while walking or running after (or in front of) a subject. In practice these are rarely used in conservation films – they are expensive and usually involve hiring a specialist

Steadicam operator. There are, however, increasing numbers of more affordable gadgets available to steady your camera while hand-holding and moving, including 3-axis gimbals and stabilisers such as Ronin and MoVI.

Cutaways

These are shots that interrupt continuously-filmed action by inserting a view of something else. They are extremely useful in the editing process – always get a few cutaways when filming in the field. They can help avoid problems during editing such as jump cuts – when a moving subject in the frame appears to jump to a new position at the edit point. Cutaways can also be used between sequences to help change the subject. Examples might be a close-up of a flower, a view of a stream, the sky, a tree, the landscape and so on.

Time Lapse

Sequences where time is compressed, known as time lapse, are increasingly popular in documentaries, especially as they can now be produced in High Definition using even basic DSLRs as well as other cameras like GoPros and dedicated units.

Using time lapse entails setting up the camera to take a number of frames (stills) at certain intervals – for example once every ten seconds. When played back at normal speed (25fps) a few hours of stills will be condensed into a few seconds. This is very effective for sunrises, sunsets, clouds scudding across a sky etc., all of which make great cutaways for your film. It is also used for sequences showing flowers opening, snails crawling, caterpillars eating a leaf, maggots devouring a carcass, stars moving across a night sky and so on.

Some cameras come with time-lapse software built in, some allow you to download a simple time-lapse program, and others will require you to buy an intervalometer. This is a simple and inexpensive gadget that plugs into the remote socket of your camera (and can also be used as a remote shutter release). You programme the intervalometer to tell the camera to take an image every x seconds for y length of time. X and y will be determined by how long you want the final sequence to last (rarely longer than ten seconds), and how long the activity itself lasts. For example, to film a sunrise you might shoot a frame every ten seconds for half an hour or so; or for clouds moving across a stormy sky, one frame every second for four or five minutes.

Set your camera on a tripod, or wall, or somewhere stable. Make sure it is set to full manual control so it cannot automatically modify any setting part-way through the sequence. Adjust the aperture and shutter speed for correct exposure, but note that shutter speeds can be set longer than you normally would for a still image (1/4 second for example) – this can create slight motion blur, which some film-makers favour, on anything moving rapidly in the sequence. This technique is known as *dragging the shutter*. Set manual focus and take a single test image to make sure exposure, composition and focus are as you want them. Then trigger the intervalometer and stand back while the shots are taken.

The result will be a number of stills (250 for example) that then need to be stitched together to make a short movie that can be imported into your video editing software and treated like any other clip. Some video editing programs can do this for you, but alternatively there are many free programs available, for both Windows and Macs (just Google 'time-lapse software') as well as some affordable software with more advanced features such as 'deflickering'.

If you want to try more advanced time-lapse sequences you can take several versions and edit between them -- using different angles, or multiple cameras. You can also use motion control rigs that very slowly move the camera throughout the sequence, giving the effect of a gradual pan or tracking movement. These rigs can be quite expensive, so they may need to be hired in for a shoot. There are a few companies that specialise in extra equipment for time-lapse shooting, including intervalometers: fastforwardtime.co.uk.

Listed in the Further Reading chapter is an excellent book that describes these methods in far more detail, and covers more advanced techniques.

Aerials

The ability to film from the air can be of great benefit to the conservation film-maker, and this has been revolutionised recently with the introduction of remote-controlled drones that can carry small cameras. Previously the only way was to hire a helicopter or small aircraft and film manually from there – a costly activity.

The most popular drones for filming are based on remote-controlled helicopters but with a larger number of rotors, often 4, 6 or 8, which confer stability and manoeuvrability. Some models, such as the DJI Phantom series, can carry

85

cameras such as GoPros, whereas larger ones can lift DSLRs. This is a rapidly-evolving area of technology and many useful extras have been developed, such as cradles for moving the camera remotely, gimbals for smooth-shooting, global positioning  systems to send the drone to specific places, automatic return-to-base programs, and headsets (video goggles) so that you can view the picture being shot while controlling the drone.

If you have not used drones before you would be advised to hire one with an experienced operator for an important shoot. It takes a lot of practice to fly a drone well and there are other considerations such as licenses, flight plans, notifying various authorities etc. These will vary depending on the location and the country you are flying in – so do check well in advance. A specialist will be able to handle all these matters for you – such as Flying Monkey Films: flyingmonkeyfilms.co.uk.

An inexpensive way to get started with aerials is to try a smaller quadcopter based on toy copters (the smallest are known as micro-drones). Some are small enough to land on your outstretched hand. Models are available with tiny clip-on cameras that record video on to a micro memory card. The better ones can carry a tiny gimbal to stabilise flight (and therefore picture) and stream live video to your iPhone (which you can wear within a simple headset which lets you monitor what the camera is seeing). With their limited range and battery life, the picture quality will not be as good as the larger models offer, so these may not acceptable for a television production, but improvements are being developed all the time; in any case they are an amusing way to practise flying skills and get a taste of aerial photography.

Filming from the air, apart from giving you interesting perspectives to add to the edit, can be used to film in dangerous situations and where access by foot is limited. Footage gained in this way, as well as being used in movies, is also increasingly being used by conservationists in the field. For example, it is valuable for surveying forests, looking for certain animal species or tree-logging activities, which would be far more difficult and time-consuming to do from the ground.

Interviews

It's quite likely that you will want to include interviews with people in your documentary. There are two main options for filming them:

1. **Without showing an interviewer** – this is the easiest option, but you need to brief your interviewee that they must include the question in their answer. For example if you ask them "How many years have you been working as a ranger?" they may simply answer "Five", which won't be easy to work into your film! Make sure you get the answer you need – ie "I've been working as a ranger for five years".

2. **Showing an interviewer** – even if you are including a separate interviewer to ask the questions, you don't necessarily need a second camera. First record the interviewee answering the questions, then record some 'noddies' – over-the-shoulder shots, from behind the interviewee, showing the interviewer nodding in interest as he or she pretends the interviewee is speaking. Finally, turn the camera on the interviewer and record him or her asking the questions for a second time – the interviewee does not of course need to be there for this. These three types of shot will edit together well and create a better viewing experience.

In both types of interview it also pays to record a number of cutaways to break up the monotony of looking at the same shot of the interviewee talking at length. Classic examples are close-up shots of the hands gesturing as he/she speaks, or a wide shot of where the interviewee is sitting/standing in the landscape/room. Again, with a single-camera setup, these would be recorded after the main interview.

One other point with interviews or when filming faces is that if they are shot against a bright sky you will find their faces are under-exposed – ie too dark. To get round this you need to adjust the manual exposure on your camera, or shoot them against a darker background – a tree for example, or light up their faces. The easiest way to do this outdoors is to use a reflector. You can buy special reflectors for this but they are easy to make with a large piece of white card or fabric – or cover a piece of card with cooking foil for an even brighter reflection. Place this out of shot to reflect sunlight into the face, adjusting the angle carefully to achieve the desired effect. The reflector can be held by an assistant, or simply propped up on the ground. If you have LED video lights, they can also be used of course: they are especially useful if shooting indoors.

87

An over-the-shoulder interview. In this case Ritish Suri is being interviewed about the wildlife at Corbett National Park in India

Presenters

If your film is to feature one or more presenters then you need to establish how they will appear beforehand, and stick to this protocol throughout the film. For example, will they speak directly to camera or to someone (often the producer or director) who is just off-camera? Will their lines be learnt, on autocue, or improvised? Will the presenter be static, walking, or in a vehicle?

Whether a director is involved depends on the budget and the size of the production. The crew may simply be the camera operator and presenter working together as a minimal team in the field.

Recording the voice of a presenter (and interviewee) is discussed in the next chapter.

Logging

This is not the favourite task of many camera operators, but it's a very good practice to get into if you are planning to edit your footage into a film. Logging in the field is usually done by the camera operator or assistant in the evening after a day's filming.

It involves in viewing all the footage recorded that day and making notes for each shot to help in the editing process and keep track of what useable images you have captured. On paper (or in a laptop/tablet database) start by stating which card or drive you're logging (eg P Warren – Tiger Poaching – Card 6 – October 2015). The three most important pieces of information to log are:

1. An identifier of the **Shot**. This will depend on which camera model you are using and how it records the footage. If it records on to a memory card or drive then it may be a simple number but is more likely to contain some other notation for the specific camera. For example, a Canon DSLR recording on to an SD card as QuickTime Movie Files may label a shot as MVI_7429.mov. When you note this also add the length of the shot (eg 06.34 (minutes.seconds)). If you are using tape then your identifier will be the timecode of the shot (known as SMPTE timecode) – eg 00:22:45:00 – 00:23:00:00 – which gives you a position on the tape in hours:minutes:seconds:frames. Most camcorders that use tape will record timecode along with the picture and sound and give you an option to view the timecode when reviewing/logging your shots. In the above example we know the exact position on the tape we are referring to and that the shot we are describing is fifteen seconds long.

2. The **Subject** of the shot – eg *mid-shot -- Ritish Suri talks about the temporary closure of areas of the National Parks by the government.*

3. The **Quality** of the shot – an important note to yourself or the editor for later such as *out of focus do not use,* or *good cutaway,* or *excellent close-up – use this …*

P Warren – Tiger Poaching – Card 6 – October 2015		
Shot	**Subject**	**Quality**
MVI_7429.mov (06.34)	*mid-shot -- Ritish Suri talks about the temporary closure of areas of the National Parks by the government*	excellent interview -- use before and over scenic shots of the Park

Labelling

It may sound obvious but I can't stress enough how important it is to label your DVDs, drives, memory cards etc. At the very least annotate each one with your name, an identifying number, the date of filming and subject area – this discipline will save time and frustration when editing, and help prevent you overwriting important originals.

Backing Up

You will have spent time, effort and money to collect your footage, so it vital to plan how you will back it up in the field in case your cards, drives or tapes are lost, damaged, stolen, confiscated, accidentally overwritten etc. This is another task often done after each day's shooting.

If your camera records on to SD cards, for example, you could copy all the rushes on to a larger drive(s) or on to other memory cards (clones), carefully labelling these so they don't get mixed with the originals. Ideally these backups will then be stored in a different place from your main equipment, or by a different member of the team. If the material is sensitive (and likely to be confiscated) they should be stored somewhere secure or even regularly posted/sent back home.

If you are backing up files from your camera note that it is important to copy the whole folder structure from the card and not just the video files (there's lots of essential but seemingly-unintelligible files in there you can't afford to ignore) otherwise the editing program may not be able to read the files properly.

As digital media storage is relatively new it is hard to say how long the data will last on them. So if your footage is valuable it's a good idea, once home, to make further backups, on different media, and again store these at different locations. Hard drives can fail if not used for some time, so even if you have a number of full backup drives in storage they should be plugged into a computer and fired up every few months to keep them in good condition.

Recording Sound

In the production of documentaries the importance of the sound track is often over-looked. It's not until the edit stage that inadequacies in the initial sound recording come to light; better to be prepared, and ensure you record as much as you can in the field. The successful recording of sound, and the creation of the film's soundtrack, is a crucial and major part of the creative process.

Ideally your crew would include a dedicated sound recordist, with his/her own specialist kit, to work alongside the camera operator. If the budget/situation does not allow this, the sound can be recorded by an assistant, the producer or, more likely, by the sole camera operator. Whoever records the sound, it is recommended that they have had some specialist training in audio skills, which will lead to better choices of recording equipment and an improvement in results.

Key Sounds

These are the individual sounds, often recorded in sync with pictures, such as a person talking, a lion roaring, or a gun firing. They typically involve the sound coming from one point source, and so can be recorded in mono (one track) using a directional microphone pointing at the source, though often in practice they are recorded in stereo (two tracks) using whatever microphone system the camera or recorder has. If movement is involved, such as a vehicle speeding past, then stereo would be the preferred option.

Atmospheres

Also known as *wild tracks, buzz tracks, room tone* or *ambience,* these are usually recorded in stereo and are the sounds of the environment – whether a rainforest at night, a busy market place or a near-silent desert.

Note that an atmosphere could be any volume from extremely quiet to very loud, the defining factor being that it has a low dynamic range – ie there will not be much difference in overall level (volume) between the loudest and quietest sounds. These tracks are very important in the editing process: whereas background sound gathered by the camera would be likely to change abruptly at each video edit point, atmospheres, used under a series of video clips, can tie the sequence together.

Whatever situation you are in, make sure you record plenty of atmospheres for use later in the editing stage. Three minutes is a good length to record in any location, and will give you plenty to play with in the edit. Unless specifically required, there is no need to record hours of similar atmospheres as, apart from taking up memory space, they will take longer to search though later. Get into the habit of recording three-minute atmospheres at every filming location after you have collected the video shots you need.

Stereo or Surround

You should know in advance whether the film's soundtrack will be in stereo or surround sound; this will be stipulated by the broadcaster if it is a film for television. Surround sound systems with five or more channels are becoming increasingly sophisticated, but it always has to be remembered that many viewers will still watch the film in basic stereo using the built-in speakers of the television, computer, tablet or mobile phone.

The most common surround sound set-up is known as 5.1 (front left, front right, centre, surround left, surround right; the .1 refers to the low-frequency effects (LFE) channel). This LFE channel is often (but not always) fed to the subwoofer speaker in a surround system. There are other systems available, with many more channels, that we shall certainly hear more of in the future. There are some specialist microphone systems, with a multi-capsule array, that will feed multiple channels. These are especially good for recording surround atmospheres, but in fact a lot of surround sound is created in the studio at the edit stage, where certain sounds are directed to the various channels. It's good practice to keep the key sounds, such as the presenter talking, to the centre.

Unless you have a multi-channel microphone system you are likely to do most of your recordings in the field in stereo or mono. If your work is destined for a surround sound production, you will record some additional sounds as you go along to be used in the edit for the surround channels. Whatever the situation, as far as you can, it's a good idea to plan ahead and make a list of the sounds you need, just as you might shot-list, or storyboard, a movie.

Sound can either be recorded directly into the camera or on to a separate audio recording unit. Let's look at these two possibilities in more detail:

Recording to Camera

Most film-makers start by just capturing whatever sound there is through the camera's microphones as the picture is recording. This can pose a couple of problems: microphones that are built in to cameras are not often of a high quality, and the camera unit is rarely the best position for the microphone. It can easily pick up camera-handling noise and the breathing of the operator, and it is likely to be too far away from the source of the sound. Ideally the microphones will be as close to the sound source as possible without causing any disturbance.

With some cameras you can mount a higher quality microphone, or, even better, plug in a longer cable to enable you to place the microphone in a better position. If the crew has a dedicated sound recordist then their mixer/recorder (or microphone) can feed directly into the camera's microphone sockets (if it has them).

Most digital video cameras can record high quality stereo sound along with the pictures – the key is the correct choice and placement of microphones to get the best sound to start with. In any case you will also need to record some audio independently of the pictures, for use in the edit. This can still be recorded into the camera; but it is recommended that you also have a separate audio recorder in your kit.

Most cameras will default to setting the sound recording level automatically – a facility known as *automatic gain control* (AGC). The problem is that if you have a sound level that changes – such as when a red deer roars loudly over a quiet atmosphere – you will hear the level of the background atmosphere change, which can ruin the recording. So it is better to use manual gain control. If you can, always use headphones to monitor the sound as you record it so that you can check the quality as you go along.

If you are recording something loud, set your audio record levels to peak a little below distortion level (shown by a red mark/light on your record-level meter) when the loudest sound is occurring. This will give you the best signal-to-noise ratio. But if you are recording something quiet, such as a forest atmosphere, don't be tempted to boost the level to just-before-distortion; this will also boost system-generated hiss. A good way to judge is to set your headphone level to a position that sounds right with loud sounds, and then never change that output level – you will find that an appropriate record level for a quiet atmosphere will sound right in the headphones (without turning it up too loud and increasing the amount of hiss).

93

Recording to a Dedicated Unit

The technology of recording sound has developed alongside the evolution of cameras. These days audio recorders capture to solid-state chips (memory cards) or internal drives and have become smaller, lighter and ever more portable and reliable.

There is a large range of audio recorders available; many professional sound recordists use Sound Devices (or similar) units (shown above), but if the budget won't stretch this far there are many cheaper, smaller units that can record at high quality. Always record uncompressed files (such as .wav files) – don't be tempted to use mp3 or another compression, as this reduces quality of the recordings.

These smaller recorders can easily slip into a pocket, so as to be always on hand should you need to record an interview off-camera, or an atmosphere. They are sometimes called 'hand-held' recorders, but they can be susceptible to handling noise: ideally place them on the ground or on a table while actually recording.

The audio files you end up with can be imported into your video edit program and placed on to your timeline in the desired position. They can also be processed and trimmed before the import, using an audio editing program, or within many video-editing programs.

Audacity (audacity.sourceforge.net) is popular, free, audio editing software, or there is *Reaper* (reaper.fm), which can be used with an inexpensive licence, and is more sophisticated, offering excellent multi-track layering capabilities.

As with some cameras, audio recording units come with either a stereo mini-jack socket (3.5mm) for attaching microphones, or with the preferred XLR sockets. These are larger and stronger and are 'balanced' – meaning that any electrical interference picked up by the microphone cable itself is cancelled out. This is especially important if you are laying long audio cables (to a bird's nest for example). Always choose high quality microphone cables as there are some very poor quality cheap ones available which may create a noisy recording. When not in use, coil cables carefully to avoid kinks. Many of the smaller recorders come with built in microphones (often a directional pair) but they can be bypassed by plugging in superior microphones if desired.

Choosing Microphones

Ideally, as well as the microphone that came with your camera – and assuming that your camera has microphone sockets or that you have an audio recorder – you would also have a good directional microphone for key sounds, and a stereo microphone (or matching pair of mono microphones) for atmospheres. If you are using a presenter, or recording interviews, you may also wish to use a tie-clip or lavalier personal microphone which may or may not be part of a wireless system (often called *radio mics*). Greater range and freedom of movement can be achieved with wireless systems, but they can produce a poorer quality sound than a wired microphone. Such systems consist of a battery-operated transmitter, often carried in the presenter's back pocket, into which the lavalier microphone, clipped to their shirt, is plugged, the cable passing through their clothing. The receiver unit is then plugged into the camera or recorder.

When you are selecting microphones, be aware that they differ both in their construction, and in their pickup pattern (also known as the polar response pattern, ie which direction they gather sound from). The most common types of construction are:

- **Dynamic** – the microphone diaphragm moves a coil in a magnet, when hit by sound waves, producing a current. These are robust and affordable microphones that work without a power-source, but need a relatively loud sound source to create a good signal – so not the best if the subject is very quiet or far away.

- **Electret** – these feature a lightly-charged diaphragm which creates a fluctuating capacitance as the sound waves vibrate it, thereby producing a current. These are usually powered by a battery (such as a 1.5 volt AA battery in the shaft of the microphone) or 'plug-in-power' supplied by the recorder. These are more sensitive than dynamics and good for quieter sounds, but bear in mind that that the diaphragm can lose its charge with time – so don't buy an old second-hand one. Make sure the battery is delivering full power.

- **Condenser** – the same basic operation as electret microphones, but requiring a higher power of 48 volts. This is often supplied from the

95

camera (or recorder) via the XLR microphone cable and is called *phantom powering*. Not all cameras can deliver this, so check before buying a condenser microphone for yours. These are very good sensitive microphones but usually the most expensive and delicate.

The main different pickup patterns are:

- **Cardioid** – or uni-directional – picking up sound principally from the front, some from the sides, and little from the rear. Stereo microphones often have two cardioid capsules inside pointing at an angle to each other.

- **Hypercardioid** – even more directional, these gunshot (or rifle) microphones are good for recording key sounds at a point source. They can also be used to record presenters talking; but you really need an assistant to hold the microphone and keep it out of shot. Supercardioid microphones are similar, but with even more front pickup and less rear pickup.

- **Figure of Eight** – these microphones, picking up principally from two sides, can be used for interviews for example. Figure of eights can also be used in combination with a cardioid microphone to produce a signal called M&S (Middle & Side, or Mono & Side). This is good for recording a point source along with some ambience, but is a more advanced technique that requires the signal to be decoded before it can be heard as normal stereo through a pair of speakers or headphones. This can be done with software or via some mixer/recorder models.

- **Omni** – picking up sounds from all directions – a pair of these can be used for atmospheres. To do this, place them about 30–40cm apart (at either end of a coat hanger is an often-used method!). Omnis are also good as lavalier microphones for interviews/presenters as they will pick up a similar level even when the presenter turns their head. Omnis are less susceptible to wind and handling noise, compared to cardioids. Like all microphones they come in a huge range of specs and prices. If you are on a budget take a look at microphonemadness.com for good omnis at reasonable prices.

There are many ways and different set-ups for recording in stereo using two microphones, some as mentioned above such as M&S, or using two omni microphones (known as an A/B set-up, which creates a very good spatial image, but is not so good for directional use). Other set-ups include: X/Y (with a cardioid or hypercardioid pair crossed in a horizontal V shape with both mic capsules at the same point, or as close together as possible, to avoid phase problems (when a sound wave arrives at two different capsules at slightly different times there may be a cancellation effect, causing a drop off in some frequencies)). A further set-up is known as ORFT, this comprises two cardioids 17cm apart, at an angle of 110 degrees in a V shape, which creates a wider stereo image than the X/Y set up. ORTF takes its name from the Office de Radiodiffusion Télévision Française at Radio France where the system was devised. It is also known as Side-Other-Side.

Recording Voice on Location

Make sure you set up sync voice recordings (when voice and video are recorded simultaneously such as a presenter talking to camera) carefully, because with documentaries there are few solutions to badly-recorded speech, and in most situations it's difficult, if not impossible, to go back and do it again.

As mentioned already, the main choices are to use a lavalier microphone or a directional one such as a rifle hypercardioid (as long as you can get it close enough, while keeping it out of shot). The best place to aim for with a rifle mic is if you imagine the speaker has a fist in front of their mouth and aim for 'the fist'.

If you have both options then it's a good idea to use both a lavalier and a rifle mic, at the same time, recording them to two separate channels, because once a rifle mic is three metres or more away from the presenter, the poor signal-to-noise ratio may make it unusable in the final mix. If the tracks are separate you can choose between them later or mix them together to get a fuller sound.

Lavalier microphones can suffer from problems such as picking up clothing noise (especially from Gore-Tex jackets) or coming loose as the presenter walks and talks. It's essential to monitor voice recordings through headphones or you may not hear the unwanted noises/distortion. A sound editor can fix some problems later, but anything that scratches over a line of speech will render it useless.

Windshields

A really useful extra piece of kit for your sound recording set-up is a windshield. Even a light breeze blowing across the front of a microphone can produce a low frequency roaring sound that can ruin a recording. A windshield creates a space of air around the microphone that is barely moving as the wind is dramatically slowed down when it hits the shield.

They are often used in combination with a fluffy/hairy covering (known as a *wind jammer*) to break up the air current even more. There are various manufacturers of windshields – the best-known being Rycote – but they can be expensive. You can make your own based on a covered wire mesh cage, but be careful not to use any old fluffy toy material to cover this, or you may well muffle the sound too much. You can buy special acoustic material for this purpose, or re-use old loudspeaker fabric coverings.

Here a rifle microphone within a windshield is used to record Barbary apes chattering quietly in a wildlife park

Commercial windshields are available for just about every size of microphone – and that includes tiny wind-jammers designed for use on lavalier microphones when presenters are wearing them outdoors – these are sometimes known as 'furries', 'fluffies' or 'moorhen chicks'!

Even the best windshields will attenuate the signal slightly, so use them only when you need to, and certainly not indoors or in a studio.

Parabolic Reflectors

 A directional tool especially useful for recording wildlife sounds is a parabolic reflector. This focuses sound from one direction and therefore amplifies the signal greatly without producing any electrical or mechanical noise. It has to be carefully aimed at the subject, as it has a narrow pick-up 'beam'. Essentially it is a parabolic dish that has a focal point (typically four inches out from the centre of the dish), at which position you secure a microphone capsule. They are particularly suitable for picking up high-frequency sounds (they are often used by people recording birdsong) but less good at recording low frequencies. The bigger the dish, the lower the frequency that can be picked up. You may need someone to help hold and aim a dish while you are filming.

The best known parabolic systems are made by a Swedish company called Telinga, but they're quite expensive. There are other options, though. This technique is discussed in much more detail on the website of the Wildlife Sound Recording Society, which is a great source of further information about recording: wildlife-sound.org.

Using a parabolic reflector to record birds

Hydrophones

If you wish to include underwater recordings then you need a hydrophone (or two for stereo). These are specialist waterproof microphones that can be used to record sounds such as the vocalisations of whales and dolphins in the sea or sounds made by fish and invertebrates in ponds and streams. Some models are very expensive, but popular and affordable hydrophones (as  well as other specialist field recording equipment) are designed and sold by Jez Riley French via hydrophones.blogspot.co.uk.

Logging Recordings

For any recordings that you have gathered separately from pictures, it's essential to log them in the same way as you would with video clips, so that you can easily locate them in future.

This can be done in a notebook or computer by file name followed by date, location, time of day and description of the recording plus, if relevant, what equipment/microphones were used. Noting the time of day is important as, for example, the sounds of a rainforest or urban atmosphere will vary greatly as you go through the day and night.

An additional method, which always keeps the information together with the recording, is simply to speak it into the microphone at the start or end of the recording. This ident, of course, can be edited out later if the track is used in the edit. If you use this method in the field it is still important to make a master list of your recordings later to ease future searches for a specific track.

Backing Up

As with video footage, it is essential that you back up your valuable audio recordings regularly. See the previous chapter for more information on backing up, and treat the files in the same way.

Post-Production

O nce all the footage has been gathered, and the location sound recorded, we move into the post-production phase during which the material is assembled into the finished programme.

The script for the narration/voice-over will be written, either by the producer or by a specialist script-writer; music, sound effects, graphics and any other necessary material will be sourced; and the video and sound will be edited. The producer (and/or director if there was one) often oversees the editing process. This is a very important stage and the picture editor's story-telling skills will help determine the strength of the final film. If you are handling all the elements of producing a film on your own, you will find the process of editing makes you a better camera operator, and vice versa. It's essential to have a good understanding of all the other aspects of film production, even if you outsource some of the roles to other specialists.

The narration and any Foley (see later) sound will be recorded and added along with music. Ideally this will be music composed especially for the film, but it may be library music for films with smaller budgets – more on all of this later in this chapter. In larger productions the picture edit and sound edit may be done separately, and by different people, but often they are done together by the sole editor.

Lastly the titles and credits are created, and then the completed film is exported. If it is to be shown on television, the movie file(s) will then be handed over to the broadcasting engineers for preparation for broadcast. Otherwise it could be uploaded to the internet, burnt on to a DVD/BD, and so on.

Editing

There is a number of choices when it comes to hardware and software for editing. The vast majority of people now edit on personal computers, and for some years the favourite combination has been Final Cut Pro on an Apple Mac system. This is changing, though, as the programs and platforms are becoming more similar and powerful all the time, so do not get too bogged down trying to decide which system to use – at the end of the day they essentially do the same thing – so start with what you've got. Remember that computers and software programs are just tools – it's what you do with them that counts!

In fact when you buy a new computer it will come with basic video editing software loaded free: iMovie on the Mac, Movie Maker on the PC. These are excellent programs to get you started with editing and have the majority of functions needed for a simple edit, with effects, graphics and titles, and basic export options.

Editing a film about lions using Final Cut Pro

When you are ready for something more advanced you could move on to a more sophisticated program such as Adobe Premiere Pro, Final Cut Pro, Avid Media Composer, Sony Vegas, Lightworks and many more. Whatever system you use, you will find an instructional book that guides you through the editing process using that particular program will be invaluable, and save you much time trying to figure things out by trial and error. There are also thousands of free YouTube tutorials that will help you with everything from a walkaround of the interface, to instructions on performing specific tasks, as well as troubleshooting.

Your first task in the editing process will be to gather all your assets on to one drive. It is recommended that you do this on a separate hard drive from your computer's main internal one. Many editing programs save all your editing choices for a movie as a 'project'; if you also save this project on the same drive it makes the whole job easy to back up, and also easy to carry around if you need to do part of the edit on another computer at any stage. As well as the footage from your camera, the assets will include all sound recordings for the film, music, graphics and so on.

How you get your footage on to the drive will depend on the camera system you were using. For example, if you were filming with a DSLR that recorded QuickTime Movie Files (.mov) they can simply be copied from the camera's memory card to a folder on the drive. If using a camcorder that records in AVCHD (Advanced Video Coding High Definition) then the files can be transferred to the drive via the editing program. With both these options you can choose to transfer only the files you want to work on in the edit, leaving out all the bad or unnecessary takes and saving both disc space and time sorting through the clips later.

If you are using DV tape, the process is known as *capturing* and involves attaching your camcorder to the computer via a connection called Firewire (you will also see this referred to as IEEE-1394); your computer will need a Firewire video capture-card installed to enable this. Then from within your editing program you will go into *capture mode* and it will transfer the digital footage and sound on to the hard drive in real time.

Other assets can simply be copied into appropriately named folders on the drive. As you will be dealing with many different files during your edit it is vital that each file is labelled clearly, and folders organised carefully.

Most editing programs divide the screen into three main areas. The first, usually top left (although you can choose how the interface is laid out), is the **browser** where you can see all the assets listed in their relevant folders. When you first set up your editing project you will direct the program to where the assets for the film are stored. The folders where assets are stored are sometimes called *bins*, a throwback to photographic days when lengths of film were physically stored in large bins in the edit studio.

The second area, usually top middle or top right, is the **viewer**. Here you can view each clip/asset in more detail and perform various functions on it. The viewer can also show you the movie you are creating as you build it, so that you can keep checking it is progressing as you wish. Some programs have two viewer screens – one for working on individual clips and one showing the movie. Some editors actually use two separate monitors, one of them showing the movie viewer full screen. This is especially useful if you have other people wanting to check progress: otherwise the individual screen areas may be too small.

The third area, usually along the bottom of the monitor screen, is the **timeline**. This is a linear representation of your movie from start to finish, with video and sound tracks to which you add clips as you work on building the film. You can add more and more tracks as you need them, or they may be added automatically by the software as required.

Different people work in different ways. Some view all the clips first and make a rough plan on paper showing how the film will unfold. Others start placing clips on the timeline and gradually add, tweak and refine them so that the movie takes shape more organically. The approach will depend on your preference and many other factors such as the purpose or message of the film, how long it needs to be, how the story needs to build and so on. It may be that the whole film was carefully storyboarded in advance, so you have a clear idea how the edit should unfold.

Often a documentary will start with a question, problem or some jeopardy, that the rest of the film gradually resolves. When you first sit down, with an empty timeline and hours of clips in front of you, it can feel like an overwhelming task. So break it down into smaller episodes, or work it out roughly on paper first. Think in terms of creating one-minute movies (thirty of them) rather than one thirty-minute movie, to help you handle the editing – take baby steps. If you are struggling, then consider taking courses, both to learn how to operate your editing program more efficiently and also to learn some of the storytelling skills used in video editing. Alternatively, if you can find an experienced editor who is happy for you to sit in on a session and watch over their shoulder, it will be an invaluable experience.

In any case, a good start is to view your rushes to remind you of what you have to play with. If you haven't done it already, now is the time to label each clip. It may feel laborious if there are many, but the time you save in the edit later on will make it worthwhile.

If the story is strongly led by interviews and narration it is often worth starting with the audio – the visuals (or cutaways) will intuitively slot into place once you have found the story through the audio. Don't feel as if you have to start editing at the beginning of the film; you can start editing at any section of the film that you feel will come together easily. Once you have a section in place, you will have got into a flow, and gained confidence, and the rest will come together more easily. You can add empty time in advance of any clip, and insert other clips at any time, so you don't need to know exactly where your clips need to be on the timeline if you elect not to start from the top.

When you are ready to add clips to your timeline, the usual routine is to open the clip in the viewer, *trim* the clip by choosing an 'in' and an 'out' point, and then move that portion of the clip to the timeline either by dragging or clicking a relevant button. Your trim points can be adjusted at any time – the great thing about computer video editing is that nothing is cast in stone – anything can be changed at any stage. Remember that all your choices on the timeline are just references to the actual footage clips on the drive – those original clips are not being altered or moved themselves.

Discussing development of the storyline during editing

105

Analysing documentaries on television will give you lots of good tips for editing. For example:

- Let a subject walk out of frame, and then cut, to end a sequence.
- Use cutaways such as a scenic shot or close-up to avoid jump-cuts.
- Start each new scene with an establishing shot (eg of the landscape, or a time lapse of a sunrise) to show the viewer that time has passed.
- Close each scene by settling on an image for slightly longer than you would expect. This may be faded to black briefly to show that you are moving on to a new scene.
- If you are filming action, such as a chase, then be aware of which directions the subjects are going in – don't keep swapping round. It is quite possible that you recorded the whole thing in one take for fear of missing something. But in the edit you can split it up with quick cutaways (shot at a different time) to make it more exciting and enable you to cut out the unnecessary bits invisibly.

Transitions

At some point in the edit (often towards the end, once you are happy with the order of clips on the timeline) you will want to think about transitions (the joins between shots). Notice that nearly every one in professional documentaries is just a straight cut. You can use a crossfade (dissolve), or fade to black, between scenes, but all the wipes and swirly effects that come with the software will look hopelessly amateurish, and are best avoided. The exception to this is maybe the opening sequence under the titles, or the end sequence under the credits, where you can be a bit more creative without detracting from the principal visual content of the film.

Sound

When you add video clips to the timeline you are likely also to add the camera's sound at the same time (usually shown as two audio tracks (stereo) beneath the video clip). If you don't want to use this sound it can easily be 'detached' from the video clip and deleted. For example, when you put in a cutaway you are unlikely to want to use the sound that went with that – but keep the continuity of the sound from the main action going.

As you go from one clip to the next you may find a jump in the sound, in which case you will have to fade the audio out and in again at the junction (an audio transition called *audio crossfade*) to smooth it out. In any case, as mentioned in the previous chapter, you will ideally be placing a stereo atmosphere on another two audio tracks beneath the video clips that make up a sequence, to create the feeling of continuity.

106

Audio clips can be handled in the viewer in a similar way to video clips: choosing the *in* and *out* points before transferring to the timeline. Also remember that clips can be trimmed on the timeline too, which is often done when fine-tuning the audio. You can work on the sound tracks for the sequences as you go along, or leave the audio edit until the video sequence on the timeline has been finalised – whichever is the most appropriate for the project.

Editing sound tracks in the viewer

As well as the sound associated with the video clips, and any extra atmospheres and key sounds you have recorded separately and added to the timeline, you may also want to add Foley sound, music and narration. Let's look at each of these in more detail:

Foley

'Foley' sound (named after Jack Foley who established the basic modern technique while working at Universal Studios) refers to all the extra sound effects, such as splashes as you see a fish swimming through water, or the crunching as a fox chews a rabbit leg, which are created and added to the edit at the post-production stage. Usually that action is too far away or too quiet to be adequately recorded in the first place.

In a larger production you may use the services of a professional Foley artist who will have a studio full of every conceivable prop necessary to create the

107

right sounds. But for a lower budget movie you can create your own Foley sounds – apart from saving funds, it's an entertaining part of the process!

Splashy sounds, for example, are made by dabbling your hand in a bowl of water, the crunches by chewing a stick of celery into the microphone. Other classic examples are footsteps made in a box of gravel or dried leaves, footsteps in the snow made by squeezing a rubber glove full of talcum powder, and the sound of a bird's wings made by flapping a piece of material in front of the microphone.

You can record your Foley sounds either though a microphone directly into your computer, or on to your camera sound track or sound recorder and then transfer them across. You can either perform the sounds 'blind', and then match them to the visuals on the timeline, or to get things really spot on, try watching the visuals while making the new sounds in sync.

The trick is not to overdo Foley, or make it too loud in the mix – keep it subtle. Not many viewers realise how few of these sounds are recorded along with the images in productions such as wildlife movies, but just because a film is a documentary doesn't mean you can't add anything (such as an atmosphere or Foley sound) to improve the viewers' immersive experience (as long as it isn't misleading).

Music

Music is nearly always used in the intro to a film and at the end as the credits roll. Whether you use music in the rest of it is up to personal taste and the style of the production. Music can be a useful tool in building drama and tension (see the movie *The Cove*, featuring activist Ric O'Barry, for example). There are many producers who feel that the main purpose of a movie is to create emotion in the viewer, while others hate music that directs the viewer how to feel (sad violins as the elephant dies, for example). It's a highly subjective and often debated issue.

Larger productions may have a music score written and recorded especially for them by a professional composer. If your budget doesn't allow for this and you are a musician yourself, you can write and record music for your own production; if not maybe you have a friend or family member, or know a local musician, who would do this for nothing in return for the experience and showcasing their work.

The other option is to use library music – there are many providers with many different deals – for example you may pay per minute used, or buy a CD of music outright that you can use on any project. If you are buying a licence to use commercial music, the cost of it will depend on the type of production (television show, DVD release, internet etc.) and the territory (parts of the world it will be released in). Alternatively there are increasing amounts of royalty-free music available online, at no cost at all, which can be downloaded at the click of a button. The disadvantages of free music are that what you use can so easily turn up in someone else's production too, and that it can take a lot of time to find something of good quality that adequately matches what you have in mind.

However you source your music, in general try to be subtle with it in the mix – never overpower the natural sounds and atmospheres. Don't feel you have to have music all the way through.

Narration

Writing and recording the narration are skills that are not easy to come by, so you may want to collaborate with someone for this part even if you have produced the whole of the rest of the film yourself. If your voice just isn't quite right then use someone else – this could be someone you know or a professional voiceover artist if budget allows.

When writing your narration script – which you may have done before you even started filming, or may have left until just before or after the picture edit – remember it has to be a story with a beginning, middle and end. Aim for complete sentences but in language that you would use when talking, rather than if you were trying to write a literary novel. Don't just describe what the viewers can see for themselves on screen, but give extra information to add to their understanding and experience. Try to throw in some questions that will be answered later in the film – regularly giving the audience a reason to keep watching – "the young tiger is old enough to feed himself, but will he evade the poachers?" Don't feel a voice is needed all the way through – there are times when the pictures can tell a better story.

If you are voicing the narration yourself, imagine you are telling a story to someone sitting next to you as you record it. Pace yourself; don't talk too fast. Act out the part – *pretend* to be a narrator – then develop your own style. Read your script to several people before recording and get feedback.

Print out your script and practise reading it several times. Mark emphases and pronunciations on the paper as a reminder. You can either deliver your narration while watching the footage, or record it separately (known as recording 'wild') and edit and place it on the timeline later. If someone else is doing the voiceover for you then sit with them and act as director – don't be afraid to ask them to re-read sections with different emphasis or speed for example.

The narration can be recorded in a professional studio (likely if the narrator is a professional voice artist or actor) or in your own home/studio.

109

If you are doing it yourself then choose a quiet room and draw the curtains (which stops sound bouncing off the glass, causing reverberation). Make sure there are no other noises in the room such as ticking clocks or humming computers. Set up a microphone on a microphone stand (or taped to a tripod) so that when you are sitting comfortably the end of the microphone is about 10cm from your mouth. Keep your head steady but relaxed as you record. Set up your script on a music stand or table so that you can read it clearly without moving your head or turning pages. Wear headphones while recording and learn to enjoy the sound of your voice.

Another device you may use is a 'pop filter'. Whenever you say words containing 'p' or 'b' sounds you'll notice they involve a little blast of air from your mouth that can cause the microphone sound to distort briefly – known as 'popping'. A pop filter is basically a piece of fabric that reduces the air blast while allowing the sound waves through. You can buy professional pop filters very cheaply: they simply clip on to the microphone stand directly in front of the microphone.

Mixing the Sound Tracks

Once all your sound elements have been sourced or recorded you may have quite a lot of audio tracks on the timeline that have to be mixed together to produce the final stereo (or surround) sound track. In larger productions this job may be given to a specialist known as a Dubbing Mixer, but often it is performed by the main video editor.

Your editing software is likely to have a number of facilities to help you with the sound such as audio transitions and special effects. Once you have completed your first mix get some feedback – is the music too loud/quiet, is the narration clear, are the Foley sounds subtle enough etc? If you are finding it hard to get all this right then you can take a specialist course (for example Wildeye runs an Audio Post Production weekend: www.wildeye.co.uk/audio-post-production).

Text on Screen

You may want to use text on your screen: for subtitles when someone is speaking in a foreign language, or not clearly, or to impart information not covered by the narration.

Your edit program will have a facility for adding text and positioning it on the screen. This usually takes the form of a video clip that can be placed on the timeline, often on a separate video track above the main one that contains the video clips from the camera. It is recommended that you keep it simple and clear: a basic font like Arial is best, and usually with white lettering and a font size that is not too large – suitable for the size of screen the film is likely to be viewed on (cinema, television, mobile phone etc.). If it is difficult to read the text against the background then either add a dark drop shadow to the font, or place the text on a shaded area that you can create for that portion of the frame. Most editing programs allow you to have basic text, moving text, and scrolling text, as well as a number of text templates (font, colour, style etc.) for different uses.

Titles/Credits

Adding the titles and end-credits is usually the last stage of your edit. Traditionally the titles (preceding the show) just give the name of the film and then the name of the narrator if you have one. The end credits then name everyone else involved in the production and thank any people or organisations as required. Even if you have performed many or all of the roles in producing the film, avoid mentioning your name numerous times in the credits. It is more modest and professional simply to say 'Filmed and Produced by Jane Brown' for example.

When designing the style of the credits try to avoid different colours for the text as it can look amateurish (white on black is often best) and don't make the font size too big. Scrolling upwards is the favourite – check the speed is not too fast to read or so slow it drags.

There are companies that specialise in creating fancy titles, graphics and credits for films, so if you have the budget they can produce something stunning to enhance the movie. But you can also have fun creating these yourself from within your edit program.

Graphics

Other graphics you may want to use can include maps, logos, still images and so on. These can be imported into the edit program as image files (such as .jpg) and essentially treated as any other clip – placed on the timeline, trimmed to the desired length, faded in and out etc. The .png file type is a good format for still images such as logos – if you are given a logo on a white background for example, you can get rid of the background in Photoshop (or a similar program) and, when you import it, the editing software will recognise that those parts are transparent.

Colour Grading

A final procedure that may or may not be required is known as *colour grading*. This is when all the visuals are treated in order to give the film a particular feel/atmosphere, or to match clips that were shot on different cameras and have different colour hues that distract. On larger productions, especially for cinema

111

and television, this task may be performed by a specialist colour grader, but if you have shot the whole film yourself on the same camera it may not be needed at all.

You can also make basic adjustments within your editing software fairly simply and easily, for example reducing exposure, correcting white balance etc. There are also often lots of presets (in FCPX for example) which can auto-correct your images, or add a certain 'look' to all of your footage.

Outputting the Final Product

Once you are happy with the final edit, it's time to export your completed movie. You will have to make various decisions at this stage such as the type of compression to use, the size of the image, and type of file. If the production is for television the broadcaster will have given you clear guidelines for all these settings. Their engineers are then likely to process your files further to prepare them for broadcast.

Productions for cinema or television are likely to need uncompressed files, or those using a compression type that results in very high quality (and large) files (such as Apple ProRes).

If you are outputting your film for other applications such as DVD or the internet you will want to use a type of compression (codec) that creates much smaller files – a very common and excellent one being H.264. At the time of writing, the new codec H.265 (also known as HEVC: High Efficiency Video Coding) is poised to overtake H.264 with its increased compression efficiency (especially useful when dealing with large files such as those produced by 4K cameras).

When you go to export the film from the edit program you should be presented with a list of compression types to choose from. You will also be able to select the size of the final movie in terms of pixels. For example, if the movie was going on to DVD you might choose 720x576 pixels (this represents a 16x9 or widescreen format for the PAL system in Standard Definition (SD)).

If it was to be in full high definition (for a BluRay Disc for example) then you might chose 1920x1080.

If it was to be for the internet – Vimeo or YouTube for example – then you might choose 1280x720. This will produce smaller files than full high definition but still look far better than SD. It's also worth checking guidelines given online for applications such as Vimeo or YouTube which go into detail about their preferred encoding settings. After some experimentation you will soon find export settings that suit your projects.

If the original footage was shot interlaced (discussed earlier, 50i for example) then at this output stage you will also want to select a de-interlace function. This will ensure there are no spurious lines across the final movie, and also allows the video to be paused without flicker. You can de-interlace in a number of ways – by applying a de-interlace filter to each clip, by changing the sequence to 'progressive', by selecting a de-interlace setting on export, or by using software after export to convert the entire movie – this will depend on what editing software you are using and whether all, or only some of, your footage was shot interlaced.

Finally the file type is selected – the most commonly used is a QuickTime Movie File (.mov) though there are several other options that may be stipulated by the application you are aiming at. The file type .mp4 is also popular, for example – especially for uploading to YouTube and other online video platforms.

The end result will either be a file that you can upload to the internet or transfer to another drive to give to a broadcaster, or, if your computer has a DVD/BD writer, you may be able to burn a disc version of it straight away.

Reaching Audiences

Reaching your audience is obviously vital, if you want your film to make a distinguishable difference in the world. To date, very little research has been published that will guide film-makers to create the right films, in the right way, to get the required result. What is clear, however, is that it is not enough to sit an audience down in front of a film and expect change to happen; there has to be a number of conditions satisfied, such as establishing the context for the screening, choosing the most appropriate films, providing the audience with informational support, empowering the audience to take action, and finally monitoring the results to establish whether your film created the conditions for the change you wish to see.

Context

a) General Context: understanding the issues that you want to address is the foundation for successfully creating a film that will engage your audience. You may need to investigate a number of contributory elements, including:

- Environmental issues (global, national and local)
- Cultural issues
- NGO partnerships (established and pending projects, PR requirements, funding applications)
- Political issues (local, national and global)
- Legal issues (local law, national and international law (wildlife protection in particular), and tribal law)
- Social issues (health and welfare)
- Ethical issues
- Funders (corporate reputation, requirements placed upon a film-maker in exchange for funding, selection of appropriate projects, how the film will be represented by the company's PR)

b) Specific Context: understanding the target audience. Films engage audiences on many levels; they respond on an emotional and intellectual level, but also on a cultural level as members of national and local communities. When crafting a conservation film to convey a well-understood message, it's valuable to consider the demographic background and knowledge of the target audience, along with its existing knowledge and experience. Considering the following will help you to define the audience:

- Culture of the audience – how does this create barriers between them and the issues, or support conservation measures?
- Age-group – primary school/secondary school/adult. Does each group require a different message, presentation or support?
- Education – does the school curriculum support awareness-raising of conservation issues which is at an appropriate level for the school audience? Does the curriculum promote solutions locally or nationally? Exposure to the issue – what is the audience's exposure to the issue, your target species or the habitats?
- General awareness – what is the audience's awareness of conservation issues nationally or locally?
- Solutions – what is the audience's awareness of possible solutions locally or nationally?
- Can the audience access support for implementing conservation measures? In order that a community receives maximum exposure to conservation messages, all influential groups should be considered for screenings. These may include:
  - Educators/schools/universities
  - Families (especially with school-children)
  - Local community groups
  - Government officials and ministers
  - The army
  - The police
  - Farmers
  - National park rangers
  - International businesses affecting or supporting conservation measures
  - Religious groups
  - All appropriate NGOs
  - Wildlife management centres
  - Zoos/sanctuaries
  - Local and national media

Content

a) **Providing powerful communication tools**. It is well documented that animals, including humans, respond to visual stimuli in order to survive and protect themselves. The sophistication of this response in human beings allows us to appreciate subtleties of emotion, and empathise with other people and situations. Visual images convey well-understood messages across cultural divides. When language is added to a film an additional human sense is engaged, that of hearing. This increases the complexity of the visual message and should be considered carefully, lest attention be diverted away from the visual message towards comprehension of the spoken or written words. To reach the widest possible cross-cultural audience it is worth considering the following:

- It is possible to create films with images, natural sounds and music and omit a narration element
- The length of the film should be appropriate for your audience; so create different timings for different audiences
- The style of the film should be researched, to establish what will engage your audience most effectively: eg animation, entertainment, dramatisation, humour

b) Communication of the conservation message. Conservation film-makers have considered the following when creating the production and distribution of their films:

- People within a story – whom will the audience connect with most easily, and how do you incorporate this person(s) into your film?
- Local references – if you include references in your film that are familiar to your audience, you will link them emotionally to your film. Consider using a landmark or a well-known story
- Local language – using words and phrases familiar in the screening location of your film is possibly the strongest link that you can make to an audience, especially an audience unfamiliar with film as a communication tool
- Strong visual images will engage and keep your audience watching until the end of the film
- A presenter who resonates with your audience will encourage it to engage with your film. This works well, in particular, with presenters who are known and respected by members of the audience or who have authority on a subject, issue or culture
- Focusing on one species or issue (illegal logging, overfishing etc) is a good basis for a story
- The frequency of reinforcement of the conservation message during the film
- Introducing the conservation message by screening a number of different films to the same audience, beginning with a 'broad awareness' film, followed by a 'specific issue and solution' film, then a 'positive action empowerment' film
- In the case of a narrator, whether a male or female voice carries more conviction or authority – be aware of cultural sensitivity

116

- The level of cultural sensitivity among the audience; it may not be appropriate to show films with animals reproducing (sex scenes), or a particularly bloody hunt, to very young children
- Music is very evocative; it can build drama, create mood, and support visual images. Music recognised by the audience creates a familiarity response; music local to the audience's country/community can bring an unexpected dimension to your film and open awareness to other cultures
- A translator may be required to facilitate the screening programme if your film is distributed in more than one country
- How your film encourages local, regional or global solutions to the issues faced by the audience
- Linking your films to local action groups, to prompt associated new projects
- The number of people in a community who need to be given the information to raise community awareness
- Whether your chosen method of film distribution encourages, or inhibits, awareness raising and solution promotion
- If the screening of your film needs to be a solo activity, or to be incorporated into other activities such as drama or music festivals. A more extended programme of activities may encourage greater participation
- The age-group or educational status of your audience may alter the way you make the film
- Consider the sustainability of your screening programme – you will need to satisfy a demand, manage the expectations of other possible screening venues, and build your capacity to deliver future programmes.

Screening Programmes and Logistics

Screening programmes are being used increasingly as part of a package of awareness raising, educating and training measures implemented by NGOs as part of their conservation activities. Many screening programmes are restricted to films that are readily available, rather than using bespoke films about the particular habitat, issues, species or contexts relevant to the areas in question. Screening programmes can be implemented on behalf of one organisation or a partnership between associated NGOs, government bodies, educators etc. In all cases a clearly-defined screening brief enables each contributor to participate effectively. A comprehensive screening programme brief may involve:

- Recognition and identification of the issues to be targeted
- Aims and objectives agreed by all partners in the programme
- A team identified and responsibilities approved by all participants
- Locations of screening programmes agreed with all venues
- Completed pre-visits to locations as required, to engage communities and field partners

117

- Schedule and timetable agreed with partners
- Appropriate films chosen for the screening programme
- A budget created and approved by funders
- Funding route agreed with funders and actioned
- Legal requirements actioned, copyright licence for screening the films received, location approval received in writing and any permits for filming endangered species received and all required terms actioned
- Health and safety elements of the screening assessed and all reasonable safety measures put in place
- Monitoring and reporting requirements agreed with partners and funders
- Training of the educators delivering your screenings if necessary
- Invitations to your target audience repeated at least twice, to ensure communication has been effective
- Media and PR invitations to maximise the impact of the content included in the screening.

Logistics

Screening programmes take place in a variety of venues and locations, some of which present more logistical challenges than others. Logistical challenges to consider:

- Locations may have full access to power, access to intermittent power, or no power at all. Power can be provided when required using generators or pedal-powered cinemas (via a dynamo)

- Venues can be overwhelmed by the number of people wishing to attend the screening. Consider possible overcrowding issues

- How your audience approaches a venue will contribute towards its overall experience of the programme; eg a screening in an open street will create a different ambience from a screening inside a luxury cinema

- Screening facilities will vary in sophistication and may need to be enhanced. If your screening programme has access to few or even no facilities you will need to consider the following:

    o Windows are often not covered in hot countries: they may be a hole in a wall, useful for ventilation but not for viewing films that require darkness. In this instance blankets, sheets, discarded doors, floor mats and pieces of fabric are all useful for creating the right conditions for screening

118

o Seating can be a challenge in many venues, primarily due to the demand placed on the building by the prospective audience size. Sheets, mats or fabric on a floor can suffice if no benches or chairs are available, and if it is possible to squeeze more people in

o Projectors and other equipment should have a clear area around them as excited audiences creep closer to the screen. The space required will depend on the equipment you are using to screen the films. Digital projectors attached to a laptop, tablet or mobile phone will require less space than a generator attached to a full-sized room projector.

- Health and safety for the audience; owners of the venue and the screening team have to be assessed and balanced with the understandable desire to cram as many people as possible into the venue. It is safer to do more screenings than to injure individuals or cause damage to property

- Transporting your screening equipment to the venue may require additional resources or logistical support, especially if you are travelling by a combination of transport methods; eg a riverboat followed by trekking, bicycle or motorbike followed by a local bus

- External noise factors can interfere with the effectiveness of the screening and it may not be possible to control the unwanted sound. Having a robust sound system will at least give you a chance of the film being heard by the audience.

Pre-visit to target audiences

If you are screening films to established communities such as schools it will be necessary to make a pre-visit to the appropriate authorities (education department) and to the head of the school to explain what you would like to do and why. This action has a number of benefits: it creates partnership at different levels of the education system and gives you an opportunity to develop a programme of screenings that can have an impact at a local level. In Uganda the Chief Education Officer was so impressed by the effectiveness of a screening programme about great apes he agreed to have local teachers trained in environmental awareness issues that could be resolved by initiating projects at local schools (see GAFI case study later).

Your pre visit would aim to:

- Introduce the screening programme, schedule and logistical requirements
- Liaise with a designated contact person

119

- Discuss all organisational requirements that would allow the screening to take place
- Answer any questions from the venue organiser or community
- Identify your target audience and discover the number of participants, their age-group, screening timescales and the method by which the audience is invited
- Assess any health and safety issues that need to be addressed
- Agree with the contact person(s) how the monitoring procedures will take place and which monitoring method is most appropriate
- Agree any associated projects with your venue partners that may be integrated into the screening programme; such as tree-planting, surveys of habitats or species, bee-keeping or cane rat-farming

Inviting guests from the local or national media will give you an opportunity to explain why the screening is taking place and encourage a wider audience to participate in any follow-up screenings or projects.

Screening opportunities

Public places

Wherever people meet there is an opportunity to make a difference. Screening your films in unexpected places can reach an audience that might otherwise be left out of traditional forms of communication, and can bring phenomenal results. You may be able to find opportunities where a 'captive' audience comes together, composed of travellers on a long journey for example. The riverboats passing up and down the Congo, for example, have two kinds of audience: the fast boats have wealthy passengers and the slow boats (which visit more locations) have a less prosperous clientele. Both these groups are important audiences for the screening of conservation films about great apes, illegal logging and bush-meat. The only variable is the way the films get shown to each group (using a DVD player and wide-screen television on the fast boat and a generator, a DVD player and a white sheet on the slow boat) and how the message of the film is supported by on-board educators (on the fast boat there is a high literacy rate, so written materials could be used; but on the slow boat the best information would come from a talk or discussion between the educator and the passengers at the end of the film). Alternatively there may be places where 'transient' groups gather for a short time. Screening programmes have been successfully operated in karaoke bars in South-East Asia and marketplaces in Kenya. However, be aware that wherever you initiate your screenings, you may need to include informational support such as educators and leaflets so that the message of your film is understood by the audience and it is not seen as just entertainment.

Events

Events often attract huge crowds, giving film-makers a chance to offer their films to the organisers and thus creating a 'win-win' opportunity. The organiser receives a film(s) to add another element to his or her event and the film-maker has the chance to screen his or her film to a mass audience. This can work especially well if your film contains a connection to the topic of the event; eg at the final of the African Nations' Football competition you might screen a one-minute film, on the surrounding huge screens, featuring members of the team highlighting the message 'Say No To Bush-Meat'. Imagine what a powerful effect this would have on the crowd! Don't be afraid to create your own event if necessary.

Politicians

Screening films to decision-makers and politicians can offer a direct route to change. It is quite a challenge obtaining access to people who have the power to create new laws, enforce existing laws, create protected areas or implement conservation strategies. Local decision-makers -- such as community leaders -- are easier to approach using local protocol, but ministers in government and presidents are surrounded by staff who often act as a filter to stop communications reaching the 'top'. To try and breach this political defence it is worth partnering with your NGO contacts who are likely to have an established relationship with senior politicians and may understand the appropriate route to reach them. Be realistic and pragmatic; you will need to provide evidence to the decision-maker that making the change you are proposing in your film will have a clear benefit, not just to the subject of your film, but to the politicians themselves.

Road trips

Mobile education vehicles can take your screening programme directly to your audience. This is especially helpful when contacting remote communities or identified target groups such as palm oil plantation owners who would typically avoid such screenings. Many NGOs have mobile awareness programmes that can be supported by your films, thus helping to increase the projects' effectiveness. It is also possible to encourage local NGOs to implement specific screening programmes. The benefit of this would be to mitigate a particular problem that is being addressed by the NGO. This might involve screening a training film to particular villagers to teach them the benefit of planting chilli borders around their village to preventing crop-raiding by elephants or chimpanzees.

Screening equipment, like projectors and sound systems, is cumbersome to carry to a venue, and presents a challenge unless you have access to a vehicle. Questionnaires and associated information packs take up a lot of space and can compound the logistical problem. Solving the problem by using a vehicle is helpful, but not perfect: one needs to balance increased accessibility against the cost of providing the vehicles, and the carbon cost to the environment.

Theatrical

Audiences across the globe flock to the cinema to be entertained and see their favourite stars in action. Inside a public theatre, the audience enters a world of drama that keeps it absorbed for hours. Yet there is no drama more riveting or engaging than the struggle we have to protect our world for our families and for future generations. We have to tell our story in a way that entertains the movie-going audience but informs and empowers it at the same time. Films that have succeeded in this endeavour include *The Cove, Virunga, Drowned Out, The Age of Stupid* and *Sharkwater.*

Film Festivals

Screening to your peers at film festivals is an indirect way of spreading your message, and gives you the chance to inspire other film-makers to tackle similar subject matters. Success at film festivals can open the doors to bigger screening platforms such as broadcast or theatrical release, and could prompt publicity for the film and its message. Festivals to consider are:

- American Conservation Film Festival – USA http://conservationfilm.org
- Environmental Film Festival – USA www.dceff.org
- International Wildlife Film Festival – USA www.wildlifefilms.org
- Japan Wildlife Festival – Japan www.naturechannel.jp
- Jackson Hole Wildlife Film Festival – USA www.jhfestival.org
- Wildscreen Festival – UK www.wildscreenfestival.org
- NaturVision Film Festival – Germany www.natur-vision.de

There are many other good film festivals of course, some of which specialise in particular animals like birds, or environments such as marine. For a list of festivals see www.wildlife-film.com/festivals.html.

Educational Establishments

Schools, universities and wildlife management centres all present opportunities to the film-maker for establishing a screening programme. In some parts of the world this will be the first time the children, students, teachers and parents will have seen a film, so the effect can be very powerful. Putting knowledge into the hands of the next generation can empower them to create a sustainable world for themselves and their future families. Expect a wide range of abilities and basic learning in your audience, whose members can range from the illiterate to those educated to university level. Therefore, matching the content of your film(s) to the audience will be a prime consideration; you may need to use educators and supporting materials to interpret the content to the audience especially if the film is screened in a language unfamiliar to them.

Films may be watched by people who have a disability; many successful screenings have taken place at blind and deaf schools where, with the help of an interpreter, the children participate fully and answer as many questions about the films as non-disadvantaged children. A film with a message that corresponds to aspects of the curriculum may encourage education establishments to participate in your screening programme, especially if there is a practical component that could be included such as planting trees, collecting litter or creating a wildlife club. Educational screenings can present unexpected challenges as you are unlikely to be able to reach all of the schools in the region at the same time. Careful planning and good communication can prevent rivalry between schools but be aware that once a successful programme is in operation, the demand from other schools to be included in your next schedule will increase greatly.

Broadcast

Television channels vary enormously across the world. In the West there is a growing number of established channels that include wildlife, nature or environmental issues in their regular programming. In other parts of the world the emphasis, primarily, is on entertainment and news, so there is no platform for films that support conservation. It may be no coincidence that the countries who have no televised education about environmental concerns are often the countries who need it most. Such content can be offered to the channels for nothing in the format they require. Broadcasters will, on occasion, require a fee for airing your film, but if you can get sponsorship or financial support to achieve this, you may reach millions of people. Africa and SE Asia are especially open to screening fee-paid films, but to maximise any benefit from the broadcast you may need to use subtitles or dub the films in the language most common in the region. If you do manage to have your film accepted by a broadcast channel, promote the air-date to as many people as possible using as many communication methods as possible, especially social media.

Radio

Local radio covers a wider audience than television in many countries and is a valuable communication route, especially if you can secure a regular contribution to an established programme or create a permanent show on the radio station. The advantage of local radio is its immediacy (it is 'content-hungry'; ie it uses a lot of material in a short time, and therefore constantly has to seek new material) and it has the ability to connect with the specific audience in the region by airing information, music, discussions, news reports etc that are all locally relevant. At the very least, radio is a useful way of promoting a screening event or activity, especially if the radio station is willing to send journalists to interview contributors to the event.

Social Media

People-power is nowhere more evident than in the area of social media, and if you can harness this grassroots passion and excitement you will have a global audience that can initiate change at a fundamental level. Factual films are viewed on all social media platforms, so there is a lot of opportunity to reach your audience. The main challenge, however, is that every person who operates a camera is effectively a film-maker, which results in a lot of films being posted on social media. Your own films will need to cut through this plethora of material and fight for the audience attention; allocating time to discover ways of driving your audience to your site, in order to view your films, is part of the challenge.

If the film material you post on social media is memorable, then people will want to share it with others. Remember, though, that internet connectivity can vary throughout the world, being very poor and intermittent in many regions; so if you provide high-resolution films on social media they may be impossible to view. Reaching as many people as possible is important for conservation organisations who will, in some measure, depend on support from other people in order to achieve their goals. Needless to say, if you can't raise a crowd, it will be hard to succeed at crowdfunding!

Harness social media -- there are many good reasons to do so:

a) You can access free platforms that have far-reaching influence on communities or even countries that may not have been reached before by films about conservation or environmental issues
b) You can 'listen' to people's thoughts and insights. It is very useful information to know how your audience is responding to issues or your film, and even negative feedback is valuable information

124

c)   You can generate leads that may result in commissions, collaborations or an invitation to screen your films

d)   You may attract people to your website who will want to use your films in their conservation work

e)   You will be contacting your audience on a personal level and building relationships

f)   When you have a strong relationship with your audience you can 'reward' its members, inspiring them to create or continue their positive behaviours; eg offer your followers special viewings or discounts on your next DVD

g)   Many people's decisions about what films to view are based on what they see on social networking sites.

Social Media Sites

New technology is being created all the time, so you will need to track new opportunities to reach your audience as they change their communication preferences. Visual media are the 'kings' on social media sites; audio is harder to comprehend on many platforms so your images will need to work hard to engage the interest of your viewers, especially for the first frame – capture the audience's imagination or intrigue them and they will follow you to the end of your film.

a)   **Facebook** is the number one social media site at the current time, and presents film-makers with an opportunity to share visual content with their own 'social community', giving viewers a chance to respond to the content of the films posted and take action should they want to. Most visual content on Facebook is at the 'entertainment' end of the spectrum but this doesn't mean it has to lose power; short films using humour, unusual activities etc will be the approach that is most popular with users and, therefore, effective. For example, in 2014 some SuperBowl adverts were seen by on Facebook by more people than saw them on television.

b)   **YouTube** hosts more videos than any other site at present. More than one billion users visit YouTube each month, watching six billion hours of video. Uploading your films to such a popular site means you can reach an impressive number of people across the world, but the downside is that individual films can be lost amid the variable quality and quantity of films that make up the site content. One hundred hours of video are uploaded to YouTube every minute. The way that content is structured on YouTube is a barrier for copyright, and protection of your material is difficult as it is almost impossible to control access and sharing of your work. As a 'free to use' site YouTube creates its income by placing adverts around your films:

125

you need to accept that, if you use a free service, you are not really the user; you are part of the product.

c) **Vimeo** is a more selective site than YouTube, and has the advantage of being perceived as having stronger visual content because of its stricter organisational control. There are robust privacy controls, and no advertising overlays, on Vimeo so there is a much better chance of a user watching your entire video: they will not have their viewing experience interrupted by the requirement to watch adverts or have to deal with banners popping up during the viewing process. As a result, the providers of content to Vimeo are more likely to be serious video creators and the audience may be more likely to watch on a regular basis. Films posted on Vimeo typically receive a high level of viewer comments with associated constructive feedback.

d) **Twitter** is growing in popularity all the time and is frequently used as a news platform. If you are filming an issue or a live event it is possible to 'tweet' pictures and video taken at the location, which provides a powerful way of bringing the event to life for those watching the situation unfold on the Twitter platform. Be careful what you say, how you say it, and focus on what your goals are for the chat afterwards, after all, live tweeting is a multi-way conversation.

e) **Flickr** – a lot of NGOs have started to use Flickr to increase their visibility online. Flickr allows NGOs to upload their photos to the site, which supports an active community of people sharing and commenting upon each other's content. Via Flickr you can tell the story of a cause supported by an NGO or highlight the issues and solutions the particular NGO may be involved with. Film-makers can start a Flickr group (which could be private or public) and use it to encourage everyone who joins the group to comment and give feedback on the photos. Camera Rwanda is a great example of storytelling using Flickr: www.flickr.com/people/camera_rwanda.

f) **Blogs**. These are a way to build relationships by using regular posts to your audience, directing it to your films and supplying up-to-date information about any issues you want to highlight. This personal written account works especially well with filmed reports created in the location of the issue and can have the power of a news item; but you need to put in a lot of work to make your site busy enough to sustain people's interest.

g) **Tumblr** is a social networking platform that allows bloggers to share their posts and expand the influence of their films into new online communities.

h) **Storify** allows the upload of images and text to the Storify site and the creation of stories in a formalised way. Once stories and articles have been created they can be shared by the originator via Facebook or Twitter.

i) **Vines** allows you to highlight six seconds of footage that will engage your audience.

j) **Instagram** and **LinkedIn** are growing in popularity. Though they are usually overlooked for video use, both are able to host video material.

k) Viddler, Blip.tv, Veoh and photobucket offer additional posting or linking opportunities for video content but, if you are tempted to use these sites, ensure your content complies with the terms and conditions.

Successful use of film in social media

- **Strong Content**. One way to generate a dedicated following is to share content that has a strong storyline and visually arresting images. This can be professional-looking posts or amateur films that will resonate with the audience. The message should be clear, so establish which key ideas you want to communicate then work out which social media tools are most appropriate for distributing your message.

- Posting films which include real people engaged in real activities will give your film authenticity and integrity.

- Don't let your films just sit on YouTube: use key influencers to talk about the issues or campaign.

- People need to know when your film is due to arrive. They're unlikely find it by accident so give them notice of the delivery date and time in order to create excitement and anticipation about the imminent arrival of your film.

- Encourage your audience to create their own films in response to what they have learned from you or what solutions they come up with. This way you will make a stronger community and strengthen your core message.

- Use the power of youth. Social media is used by all age-groups, but teenagers in particular are attracted to things that inform and inspire them, especially when it enables them to shape their own future. If film-makers can engage young people in conservation issues it is possible that they may persuade their friends to help as well. Teenagers are, generally, drawn to attractive and stylish visual content, which is why films that are created this

127

way will appeal to them. Updating your social media frequently will help to retain their interest.

- Word of mouth has always been an effective marketing tool. These days it is just as likely to come from a social media website or smartphone application as from a neighbour across the fence. When consumers look up a business through a search engine they often find reviews online. If the first reviews read by shoppers are negative that can turn potential customers away. Linking your film to negative reviews about products that are harming the environment or public health could start a ground-swell of bad publicity for the companies involved. This could influence consumers, enabling them to post reviews that might encourage a company to change its policies or manufacturing methods.

- **Influencers**. Online influencers are individuals who have lots of Facebook friends, who have a large Twitter following, a blog and other social accounts like Instagram or Vine. These influencers have an audience that trusts them and by joining their networks and enrolling them in promoting solutions to the issue you are challenging you can reach a wide audience of potential supporters.

Monitoring Effectiveness

Film-makers are increasingly aware of the power that the films they produce can have over an audience. This has led to an unprecedented number of film-makers and producers donating their films to be used in film-screening programmes around the world. This support for education, awareness, legal compliance, creation of protected areas and provision of alternative environmental solutions to local issues has made a substantial contribution to the observed and documented results published by the recipients – the NGOs and organisations – who strive to change the state of the planet. However, the donation of films is only the first step along the conservation path. Films are immensely influential but, in order to create lasting change, a second step is needed: they need to be aligned with an education and support structure that will empower the audience to understand what the problem is and how they may be able to contribute to a solution. Once the first and second steps have taken place, the third step is to discover whether the films have succeeded in their aims or not. There are many stunningly beautiful films that are enjoyed by an audience but that don't make a difference to the people, issues, species or habitats featured. The only way to make this discovery is by monitoring the audience's response to the screening. So how can we monitor results?

The Information

Find ways to collect the information you will need in order to assess the effectiveness of your film or screening. The information you will need to gather will include details about the audiences, their reaction to your film(s) and conservation measures resulting. Different information collection methods will be appropriate for different audiences. These basic questions will help you to choose which method is most useful to you, and most suitable for your target audience:

a) What depth and type of information do you need to collect? Always bear in mind how you want to use the information before you collect it. This will influence what information you collect, how you collect it and how you store and process your findings. Consider your goal: if you want to create awareness of an issue, the way you collect the information will be different than if your aim is to have 100,000 trees planted in a specific area.

b) How can you check the reliability of your information? Inaccurate data are not worth gathering unless the ultimate recipient of the information is aware that this is a 'snapshot' of the study and not a conclusion. Reports will have a greater impact if they are specific; eg a report that confirms you have screened your films to one thousand and forty-two school children from eight primary schools within the Kisoro region can prove to funders that the donation they made to you was spent according to their wishes. Accurate information is by far the most effective when recording any change occurring in a situation, as it provides tangible, fact-based, evidence. This is essential in certain circumstances; eg if you want to highlight the urgency of a situation, promote specific conservation solutions, reveal the status of an endangered species, apply for grants or prove the outreach potential of your film.

c) On a basic level make sure that everyone responsible for collecting information is doing it in the same way so that it is consistent and there are no gaps. Small amounts of information can be collected on paper and analysed manually but it is likely that you will use a computer to manage and store your information.

d) How much time can you afford to spend on collecting information? This important aspect of your film-screening programme can take a lot of time in preparation, delivery and in collating and analysing the results. Factor in that different collection methods will take varying amounts of time; eg questionnaires will take more time than self-evaluation.

e) How much will it cost? Collecting information has a financial cost as well as a time cost. Even if you are just collecting the information on paper the materials will need to be paid for. This is one area that is often overlooked by film-makers when they apply for funds to carry out screening programmes.

f) How will you analyse the information? Depending upon the information you want to collect you could receive vast amounts of data that will need to be analysed and constructed into a rational presentation that is easily understood by the people it is intended for. Visual presentation using bar charts, pie charts or even custom-made graphics or animations can identify various elements of your information in an attractive and accessible way.

Collecting the information

Once you have established the level of information you want to collect you will need to decide how you are going to collect it. There are various well-established ways to do this:

a) Questionnaires and surveys are the most frequently used collection tool in the field as they are cost-effective and easy to distribute and complete. Questionnaires should be translated if necessary into the local language and support should be available to those who are fully- or semi-illiterate as they will need help to answer the questions on the form. The questions on the document(s) will be the key to finding out the information you seek, so constructing the questions in 'blocks' (grouped by topic) will help the participants to understand the questions and help the person analysing the data to assemble the information in a cohesive way. These blocks could ask questions about:

1. **Audience**: age, exposure to previous screenings or conservation projects, attitudes to conservation.
2. **Films**: you will certainly want to know what the reaction is to the film(s) screening; eg what did the participants think of the film, was it too long or too short, should a local person have appeared on screen, is it in the right language, who else should see this film?
3. **Conservation measures**: do the participants recognise any of the issues raised, was the film too long or too short, who should be responsible for finding solutions to such issues, would the participant want to help with this action?

The answers given to this suggested questionnaire will reveal whether you are screening the right films to the right audience, thus giving you the ability to adjust the content of the films, the length of the films or the audience for a particular film.

b) Observation: some aspects are difficult to record by standard recording methods; eg changes of behaviour and attitude shift, as they can take place over a long period of time. If a difference is observed in human or organisational behaviour it may be hard to link the actual change with the initial screening programme, but this does not mean the difference was not prompted by the film itself. If you notice that more families are using charcoal-burning stoves six months after you screened a film about the value of the trees in their forest and why it is important to reduce wood consumption, it may be attributable in some measure to your film.

131

Observed changes can be recorded although there may be contributory factors to be included in the results in addition to your screening.

c) Interviews: first-hand accounts by the people connected to the issues raised in your film or screening programme are a direct indicator of whether change has taken place or not. Such accounts can be recorded on film, in audio or on paper and may form the basis of the evidence that the film has had an impact.

d) Keeping records and notes: If your film-screening programme takes place at a number of venues, with different audiences and different films keep the particular results discrete rather than aggregating them. The information collected at each screening will contribute towards a more comprehensive report which can analyse change on a territory or even national level.

e) If your film has been broadcast in Europe or the USA it will be easy to obtain viewing figures as these territories published them weekly. If your film has been broadcast on other networks, the viewing figures may not be so readily available. It is possible to discover the size of the television audience in a territory through film distribution companies or magazines.

f) Internet 'hits' are an accurate way to record interest in the material you have posted. There are various analytical programs available to internet users.

g) Audience figures for a theatrical release of a film can be obtained from the company distributing the film, from the participating independent cinemas or the organisers of the festival in question.

Monitoring the information

The most important information to gather will relate to your films, your audience and any outcomes resulting directly or indirectly from your film-screening programme. In all instances you are seeking to monitor impact, considering:

a) Indicators that are specific and measurable; eg how many wildlife clubs were established as a result of screening films to a community over three months

b) Attitudes to, and perceptions of, the films people have watched

c) A measurement of what and how much information (if any) is transferred from the shown films to the audience

d) Demographic data about the audience such as hometown, school area, age, academic level

e) Exposure to previously-seen wildlife documentaries and experiences with similar environmental conservation NGOs.

f) If there is a possible 'trickle down' effect from the audience to non-audience community members through word-of-mouth and/or social observational learning

Evaluating your information

This is where the truth is revealed and you discover whether or not your goals have been fully met, partly met or if you need to reconsider key elements of the screening programme or films. To evaluate successfully you may want to consider:

a) How often you monitor – regularly monitoring information over a period of time will establish if your results are consistent, or if they include variables that may need to be examined

b) Self-evaluation of your film or screening is obviously the cheapest method for establishing results that you can use. Your declared aims for the individual film or screenings will set the criteria against which the evaluation will take place; eg do you want a certain number of people to see the film, do you want a law to be changed or implemented, do you want to cover a particular territory in a certain amount of time?

c) External evaluation may be appropriate if you lack the skill, time or confidence to carry out the evaluation by yourself. Sometimes funders will require an external evaluation of a project as a condition of their funding. An outside evaluator should be chosen carefully to ensure they have the necessary experience in film, or in screening programmes to your specific audiences. Once you have chosen your evaluator you will need to establish the criteria for the evaluation, when the report should be delivered and how the evaluator should access the information

d) Case study evaluation allows you to examine a particular individual, event or activity in greater detail. You may want to let participants tell their story in their own words, or use individual stories alongside each other to reveal the breadth of the results or to contrast differing outcomes

e) Appreciative enquiry focuses on what has worked well, often producing stories about the results in order to reveal the outcomes

f) User-led evaluation is where the evaluation control passes to the users themselves or to user-representatives. This works if you want the people who are creating the screening programmes or implementing the screenings to evaluate the results

g) 'Turning the curve' is a process that compares progress of a project and the subsequent results against what would have happened over time if the project had not taken place. This evaluation can create the biggest motivation for film-makers, communities, governments and the public who are concerned about the future we all face

Ethical considerations

These are important to establish in evaluating your screening programmes.

a) Store information in accordance with data protection requirements
b) Obtain informed consent from individual participants
c) Ensure you don't breach confidentiality
d) Observe copyright and intellectual property when using secondary materials (such as articles and other organisations' data)

Present your findings

Do this in the way that will gain you the most impact from your screenings and longer-term results. This may involve some or all of these options:

a) Formal display
b) Website
c) Local presentation
d) Discussions, talks and presentations
e) Reports
f) Analysis for funders
g) Publication

Results

It is important to communicate the results your film-screening programme or film has achieved to all of the people involved in making and distributing the film. Not only is this a considerate gesture, which acknowledges their contribution, but also it may inspire and empower future collaborative effort. If your film has featured a campaign, local issue or community, the results are particularly important to convey to the key participants so they will learn the value of their actions and understand that they *did* make a difference. Certain films will have impact over many years; others will have an immediate result. Collecting information about the status of the issues before and after your screenings will allow you to measure the difference that you have made. Some impacts are difficult to measure especially in the area of public opinion and attitudes. The accumulated impact of conservation films and screening programmes across the world is impossible to measure but individual results have been recorded which have had an undisputed impact. By evaluating your film or programme you will have achieved at the very least some of the following benefits:

a) Knowledge about how your film was received by its audiences and what suggestions they may have to adapt future films or screenings
b) Relationships with local communities can be reinforced and strengthened
c) Created demand for more screenings, information and projects
d) Awareness raised of local, national or global issues
e) Laws implemented
f) Laws enforced
g) Habitats protected
h) National parks created or extended
i) Individuals in local communities inspired to be leaders in conservation
j) Wildlife clubs established
k) Educational visits to local forests initiated
l) Sanctuaries supported
m) Wildlife corridors established
n) Species 'adopted' by local communities
o) Trees planted
p) Campaigns established

If you can prove any of the benefits above (or other benefits not listed) you will be in an excellent position to reveal your evidence to potential supporters and funders which may give the opportunity for a sustainable future to the change you and your extended team have initiated, – and that is what conservation film-making is all about. On a personal level there is an evaluation you will not read about in books or manuals, or even hear discussed professionally. This is emotional evaluation, which by its very nature is highly individualised and hence impossible to measure adequately. However, it is worth mentioning because it has an impact on the effectiveness of film-screening programmes. Many of the issues that conservation film-makers address are immensely challenging on many levels: logistical, political, financial but also emotional. Continually fighting corruption, poverty, warfare, environmental destruction, greed and cynicism is hard work and there are, naturally, times when the temptation to stop, give up and forget about it will be overwhelming. It is in those times that the results of your screenings will be of most value to you and those around you. Remind yourself of what can be achieved, that solutions can be found, and remember that you are part of a global community of committed, dedicated conservation film-makers. You are not on your own.

- - - - - - - - -

The Films That Make A Difference Project

This is a project set up in collaboration with Wildeye, Brock Initiative, Wildlife-film.com, the American University's Center for Environmental Filmmaking and Filmmakers for Conservation (FFC). The 'Films That Make A Difference' database aims to assemble an online directory of effective conservation films. This can be used by anyone looking for models for their own productions, for proof that film-making can make a difference, and we hope it will lend strength to funding applications etc. The films may have been used in many different ways: on TV, on the internet, shown locally and/or to influential people/politicians and so on. The database can be accessed at: www.filmsthatmakeadifference.org

The database is split into four categories:

1) **Films that have made a difference** – films that have been documented or otherwise proven to have made a real and tangible difference to a conservation issue

2) **Films that have contributed to making a difference** – undocumented or unproven but made about an issue that has found a degree of success

3) **Films that have a conservation/environmental message or theme** – good conservation films that will have raised awareness of an issue but scored no known conclusive successes

4) **Film-makers who have made a difference** – this category includes film-makers and organisations that have made a significant contribution to conservation film-making over time

The directory is a user-friendly database of profiles. Individual film-makers and production companies globally can provide information about their films to the directory, which is online and available for all to read. In return, those who wish to make conservation films can refer to the directory for guidance and evidential support that films do make a difference. Participating films can be of broadcast quality, or captured on a budget camera and edited on a home computer (and anything in between). Quality of production is not the priority – effectiveness is key.

Each film entry has:

- a paragraph describing the production
- a list of the positive results
- contact details
- online web links, if available
- still photo(s) from the production

When you are ready to submit your own film that has made a difference, send your information to the project manager Jason Peters: jason@filmsthatmakeadifference.org

Case Studies

In this section we look at a variety of productions, film-makers, technologies and projects all of which have used film to make a difference.

Ben Please
Film-maker
Maji ni Uhai (The Brock Initiative / FORS)

The *Maji Ni Uhai* (*Water Is Life*) film was the first I made for The Brock Initiative (www.brockinitiative.org), a project set up by veteran BBC Natural History film producer Richard Brock. I started working in 2002 after a very simply-stated request from Richard. He had a large archive of good natural history footage, originally shot for television, but now not being shown. He wanted that resource of footage to be put to use, back in the country where it was originally shot, to benefit environments that were now under threat. My job was to work out how best to do that.

I proposed to go to Tanzania, a country I knew relatively well having spent a year teaching and leading conservation expeditions there. Richard had lots of East African footage, but we approached other film-makers who we knew would have their own archives.

My challenge, as Richard would say, was to make 'a real difference, on the ground'. This is pretty open-ended when you think about all the possibilities. Do we go ahead and try to make a BIG film to reach millions? Do we pick something we're passionate about? How do we choose? I could think of plenty of things and had lots of big ideas, but it was my ignoring these big ideas that actually made *Maji Ni Uhai* such a successful film.

I was, at best, a very novice film-maker, with basic editing and filming skills. I am a pretty good storyteller, but I knew that even if I could tell a great story I couldn't, in good conscience, use a film to preach environmental actions when I didn't know all the facts or potential consequences. Film, at its best, is an incredibly powerful tool and can be very influential when the medium is used skilfully; but with that power comes the responsibility to make sure the right stories get told in the right way. I had to find those stories.

The next big lesson I learnt from Richard Brock, before I made my first film, was that making films that make a difference is not always about reaching millions of people. His career was all about reaching as many people – via the BBC – as possible, which, while highly successful in many ways, wasn't always effective in terms of real environmental benefit. Richard would say that reaching a small audience, if it's intimately connected with the problem, is JUST as valid a reason for making a film as it is to make big-budget films. Small-audience films should not be valued less, they just do different things. Even if a film reaches only one person, if it's the right person, in the right way, it can have a huge impact. That was one mantra of The Brock Initiative. His productions had hardly any budget, no time was spent on making them look 'nice', but rather everything went into making them as engaging as possible for exactly the audience we wanted to reach. Great storytelling can arise just from taking time, applying thought, and feeling empathy with your audience.

I'll illustrate the point with a 'fictional' film. Let us say you have identified an extremely endangered animal that lives in a very small area. The animal is under threat from poaching. There are five key poachers. It's easy to see that one potential approach would be to find and spend a huge budget, making a film to engage and enrage millions about the issue. Or we could make a very simple film, on virtually no budget, in a local language, designed to catch the attention of those five people, and show it in the one village where they are known to live. Both approaches are valid. The second, in our opinion, would probably have the greater impact, reaching out directly to the actual people involved. And crucially, as the second way cost virtually no money in film production terms, we could do it next week. The first way we would have been fundraising for years to get the money, by which time it could have been too late.

I've rambled on for a while about the background to what we were doing, but I think it's really important to understand the motivation and methods of what we were doing. We had an idea about *how* film could be really effective at bringing about positive environmental change, and now the task was to implement that. So, I honed my filming and editing skills as much as I could (including training at Wildeye's excellent film-making classes) and digitised as much relevant natural history footage from Richard's and others' archives, on to a hard drive. I packed a small miniDV camcorder, microphone, set of headphones, a laptop for film editing, all into my backpack and headed out to Tanzania for three months. But I didn't make any films in that time.

Instead I toured the country, setting up countless meetings – from high-level government departments and international NGOs, to grass-roots groups or even individual people in tiny villages who I heard happened to be very passionate about a particular local environmental issue. I was exposed to an amazingly diverse array of environmental concerns and initiatives, at all levels in Tanzania. The first part of my role became that of an informal auditor – making the best judgment I could as to whether the work of the organisation seemed positive, correct, honest, constructive, inclusive and good. It's all very well to claim that, as an environmental film-maker, I could somehow remain impartial – and I'll be the first to admit that I wasn't qualified to make those judgments (and I would certainly keep those judgments to myself) – but in the end I had to trust my gut, on the information I'd received, as to whether I wanted to spend my time and effort supporting, encouraging and indeed facilitating the work of that organisation or individual. Generally I found organisations and people very good, and a few were outstanding; but there were those, too, whom I would certainly have not wanted to help, even though they came under the banner of 'environmental conservation', 'NGO' or 'charity'. Those titles don't mean a thing. It's what is underneath that counts, and at the end of the day you have to trust your judgment and do your best to find out what you can.

After months of meetings I had found some exceptional organisations, and people, at all levels. The next stage was to tell those short-listed groups what I could offer them: my time and energy; the equipment and footage I had access to on my laptop; my scientific background; my fairly basic but adequate film-making skills; and also the ethos of what we were trying to achieve. I asked them to think if there was a way they could imagine a film, or a way to use footage, that would have a real impact on their activities. Many didn't, and could visualise only general fundraising films for the masses, which are fine, just not what I was offering. Just occasionally it would sync up when I found an organisation I could get passionate about, and in return they would get inspired about how they could use film, in ways that they had not previously considered possible, to the direct benefit of the environmental cause they worked for.

This illustrates perhaps the most important aspect of locally-based conservation film-making. That the idea for the film, the motivation, the real passion for its production, must come from the people who (a) know about the subject and (b) will be the ones who are going to actually be in charge of showing the film and following it up once it is made. If (a) and (b) happen to be the same person (the film-maker him- or herself), then fantastic. My hunch is that if you are reading this, you are passionate about being a conservation film-maker; you may want to make lots of films; help lots of people and issues; you enjoy film-making. That described me anyway. So I knew that if I wanted these films actually to be used, I needed to relinquish my ownership of them and instead let the motivation and direction come from those people and organisations who would actually use them. It was my job as the film-maker to bring these people to the surface, and to help steer the process: but at the end of the day, it had to be *their* film, not mine.

I hope that this introduction to the background will help you see why I chose to do the things I did. One of the first organisations to understand what I was offering was called The Friends Of Ruaha Society (FORS). The Ruaha is both a National Park in Tanzania, and also the main regional river (The Great Ruaha River) that runs through that area. The river channels water from the highlands, and the wetlands directly beneath them, through the Ruaha National Park, then through many villages and towns, via one of the country's biggest hydroelectric power plants, and finally to the sea. As you can imagine, there were countless issues regarding water use, from the source of the river in the highlands (which saw deforestation and water diversion to inefficient monocultures) to the wet lowlands (where huge cattle herds would be brought to graze, trampling the swampy ground and reducing its ability to hold water all year round). All the way down the river there were issues of pollution, people not considering the downstream effects of their usage, and also simple practical problems for the villages regarding water storage and efficient water use. The biggest problem of all was that The Great Ruaha River, from once being a river that ran all year round without fail, had now stopped running – completely – for as long as nine months per year – over several years. You can only imagine the knock-on effects for wildlife in the National Park, and for all the people who live and rely on its water downstream.

 FORS are a local NGO and their remit was to work with communities around the Ruaha National Park, addressing local environmental issues, reducing conflict between locals and the Park through environmental education in schools, and facilitating access to the Park by hosting regular school trips. Together we saw many potentially useful films, but the first and biggest idea was to address water issues – from the macro problems of the Ruaha water cycle, down to the very personal water problems that people faced every day.

141

To make the film as effective as possible we considered the motivation people would have for watching it in the first place. FORS worked primarily in schools; for teachers actually to want the film to be shown it had to address the Tanzanian school curriculum, so we covered all aspects of water that they would otherwise need to teach. It had to be in Kiswahilli, as this was the language everyone understood. It had to be voiced by someone whom people knew, so we asked a local radio presenter to be the narrator. The script was written in consultation with the teachers and FORS, so they felt some ownership of that.

If we wanted whole communities to see the film, not just schools, we'd have to engage as many people as we could in the actual production of it. It's like a school play: if your kids are in it, you go and see it; if they are in a film, you bring your friends too! FORS got pupils from all the local schools to draw pictures showing how water issues affected them, and these were then shown in the film. They asked each school to write a song about water, and these pieces provided the sound track. While filming, I visited these schools and interviewed pupils from each. From these we selected the least camera-shy pupil (Faraja Mramba), and persuaded a locally-based international NGO (WCS) to donate two biplane flights over the Ruaha: we took Faraja and filmed his reaction and commentary as he witnessed the water issues from the air. It was from his own lips that we heard about downstream effects, or unwise water use upstream, and its visible effect on wildlife, environment and people.

We also had to consider the different ways in which people would watch the film. Sound is always an issue, so we subtitled it in both English and Swahili versions. We also cut it into different versions, from a straight hour-long feature, to multiple three- to ten-minute versions, so that the end user could mix and match the screening to support what was happening that day.

We involved and interviewed scientists from the organisations, to make sure we got the correct messages into the script. We used footage from many different film-makers, professional and amateur in the film, and I even trained up the two paid staff from FORS to film and edit with me. I basically did everything I could to make the film not mine, but all of theirs. And it worked.

The film, in its various forms, was used for many years by FORS. It toured regularly round all the schools in the area, was shown in the National Park, and from the backs of trucks and screening units. It was also shown at scientific conferences debating the Great Ruaha Problem, and was informally cited as one of the main tools for convincing government representatives finally to take action on some of the major issues upstream, such as over-grazing on the Usnagu wetland swamp, which had such a devastating affect downstream. The swamp subsequently received protective status, which saw an increase in the flow of the Ruaha River. The reason it was effective here was that it was seen as the first real local Tanzanian voice people had heard, and it has since reached a wider audience, being shown many times on Tanzanian TV. A film made by Tanzanians for Tanzanians. I was truly out of the picture, which was great.

But the thing that really made the project special for me was when, about ten years later, I was working in Kenya, running a camp training environmental organisations to make their own films, and one student had come back from a filming expedition to a local village and was showing me some of her footage. She said she had filmed a song that the children had been singing about water. She pressed play on the camera, and they were singing the title music for *Maji Ni Uhai*, one of the songs written a decade before by a local school for the film. I don't know if they had seen the film – it's unlikely – but the song from it had travelled in its own way, it had its own life, and that makes me really happy.

Shekar Dattatri
Wildlife and Conservation Film-maker
India

As the year 2000 dawned I ought to have been happy and contented. As a successful freelance producer of, and cameraman on, high-end natural history films, I was privileged to work with some of the world's leading broadcasters and production houses. Just two years earlier, *Television Business International* (TBI) had featured me in their magazine as one of the 'Top 10 rising stars of wildlife film-making'. From my simple beginning in the mid-1980s with just a spring-wound 16mm Bolex camera, I had 'made it' to where I had always wanted to be.

I loved everything about my 'job', especially the 'roughing it' out in the wild, and spending endless days watching and filming wildlife. So at the beginning of 2000 – after having successfully produced and shot another natural history film for international television, and with funding in the pipeline for the next one – I should have been on cloud nine. Instead, I felt unfulfilled and listless.

143

Something didn't feel right, although I couldn't put my finger on it. So I took a break from the high-pressure world of broadcast television, to ponder over the meaning of life. Over the next couple of months, I gradually began to understand the reason for my discontent.

Since the age of thirteen I've been passionate about nature and conservation. The career in film-making evolved from my desire to get other people equally fired up about saving what's left of the natural world. But television in the 90s was fixated with depicting 'pristine' nature and animal behaviour. The films were beautiful and fascinating, but had negligible impact on conservation on the ground. Important though such films are in their own way, I was no longer satisfied with making them, especially when nature in my own country, India, was beset with all kinds of problems.

So I turned down the commission of a half-hour natural history film from a major broadcaster – which was tantamount to professional suicide – and decided to focus my energies in another direction. By this time I had come to realise that wildlife programming was a business like any other, and there was no sense in vilifying broadcasters for churning out 'escapist' wildlife documentaries. I no longer even believed that television was the right medium through which to bombard people with hard-hitting conservation stories. Most of us watch TV to unwind and be entertained. Gloom-and-doom stories would just be banished with a click of the TV remote. So I decided to forsake broadcasting in favour of 'narrowcasting', and make well-researched films on specific conservation issues in India. These would not be for viewing by millions around the world, but for the express attention of 'captive audiences', particularly comprising local or national decision-makers who could directly make a change in policy or practice.

That was fifteen years ago. And while I immensely enjoyed making films for television, I've never regretted the decision to walk away from it all. So, what's it been like?

Well, for starters, there's no money in conservation film-making, since my 'clients' are mostly cash-strapped NGOs. Personally, I went from earning a few hundred pounds a day as a professional cameraman and producer, to not just little income, but, at times, actually spending money from my own pocket to underwrite the cost of projects or equipment. Also, from budgets of a few hundred thousand pounds per film, most of my projects have been resourced from laughably small sums of money that often barely pay for the most basic production expenses.

On the up side conservation films, while still needing to be made with the best professional skills, do not need to exude 'broadcast standard' production values in order to be effective. I shoot with whatever cameras are affordable, and edit everything on a Mac. While on location, I bunk with friends or pitch a tent. But even this approach could not have been sustained without a little help now and then. Sometimes financial assistance has come from unexpected sources: a chance meeting with a philanthropist; a proposal funded by a grant; or a cash award bestowed serendipitously.

The equally large challenge with conservation film-making is: what happens once the film is made? The most powerful film is almost worthless if it's merely uploaded online. The number of views on YouTube matter little. What matters entirely is getting the film seen by the *right* people – those who wield real influence, and have the authority to make a new policy, enact new legislation or take other kinds of action to help solve the problem depicted in a film. Since most of us, as film-makers, may not be equipped to do this ourselves, it's vital to co-opt partners who are equally fired-up about the issue, and who are willing to campaign and lobby tirelessly, using the film as a powerful tool.

Dealing with conservation issues day in and day out can sometimes be quite depressing. To avoid burning out, I practise what I call 'passionate detachment'. This is a state where, although I may have worked passionately to bring clarity to a particular conservation issue through my film, and may have presented the problem and its potential solutions in a persuasive manner, I work with the full realisation that the desired end-result is not entirely in my hands. Sometimes action can be swift and tangible, and the issue might get resolved before my eyes. More typically it tends to be a slow, long slog before anything tangible emerges. In the worst-case scenario, despite all the right people seeing my film and making all the right noises, nothing has come of it. I've learnt not to take these sorts of setbacks too personally. A conservation film-maker is merely a small cog in a very large wheel, and it's best not to forget this. So, I try to maintain a level of detachment after a film is done, and don't obsess over 'measuring' its impact, or beat myself up if results don't match expectations. Conservation is often a long road, and there is rarely any instant gratification. So it's absolutely necessary to develop the Zen-like mindset of a *Karma yogi*. That's to say, I do my best, collaborate with the right people, and persevere. But I don't go in expecting miracles.

So, after over thirty years as an independent film-maker of both big-budget wildlife films and low-budget conservation films, do I have any advice for newcomers wanting to make films that make a difference? Well, here are a few 'words of wisdom', for what they are worth!

- Since making conservation films alone will not put food on the table, it's important to mix it up. Besides advocacy films, I also make training videos, educational documentaries and short films, albeit all in the wildlife and conservation space. There are a few avenues for making non-broadcast films if you look around

- While conservation films don't need fancy production values to be effective, they will not succeed if they are sloppy. So I make them with passion and care

- I try to keep advocacy films short and snappy, as decision-makers have neither the time nor the patience to watch something that rambles

- I don't try to cram every bit of information on a chosen subject into a film, as it will result in an information overload. Knowing what to leave out is as important as knowing what to include. I believe that a film shouldn't try to be an encyclopedia, but rather a 'hook' to get a larger discussion going

- I never, ever, embellish or exaggerate, as that undermines the credibility of a film

- I don't make my advocacy films to win appreciation from fellow film-makers or awards at film festivals. My primary goal is to make them work effectively for my chosen target audience. Conservation films, in my opinion, work best when they are simple, direct and 'tell it like it is'

- Finally, I don't expect praise for my work. In fact, with every film, I brace myself for retaliation from those opposed to the cause I'm espousing, and there have been times when things have got very nasty indeed. I've learned first-hand that making conservation films can be a minefield, and isn't for the faint-hearted!

Happy film-making!

www.shekardattatri.com

Julian Newman
Campaigns Director
Environmental Investigation Agency

Since its creation in 1984 the Environmental Investigation Agency has pioneered the use of undercover investigative techniques in defence of the natural world. Its ethos remains unchanged: protecting the environment with intelligence. This involves witnessing and documenting crimes against nature, such as illicit wildlife trade, illegal logging and the smuggling of ozone-depleting chemicals.

To achieve its goals EIA deploys a range of techniques, including in-depth research and analysis, field investigations and advocacy for regulatory change. As a relatively small organisation, EIA relies on gathering powerful visual images of the impacts of environmental crime and evidence of those responsible. It has its own in-house film unit, which produces hard-hitting short films that are shown at press conferences, major meetings and by broadcasters.

As its name suggests, investigations are central to EIA's *modus operandi*. These operations are aimed at gathering evidence of how environmental crimes are carried out: for instance, revealing the smuggling routes and methods used to move poached elephant ivory from Africa to markets in the Far East, and catching some of the culprits on camera. A vital part of this work involves undercover filming.

When I joined EIA back in 1997 my first assignment was to travel to Madrid to meet a trading company implicated in the smuggling of ozone-depleting CFC chemicals. For this task I was equipped with a fake business card and a hidden camera. In those days the technology was pretty basic: a Hi-8 video camera (concealed in a bag with the lens covertly poking out) and microphone, that needed 12 AA batteries for power. Limited tape-length and battery-power meant that both tape and power had to be changed about every forty minutes, which didn't leave much time for niceties, especially if the targets were late arriving. If the meeting got beyond the half-hour mark, excuses had to be made to visit the lavatory so the battery and tape could be changed.

147

I was once in a meeting with a major ivory carving factory in Beijing, China, and had to go to the bathroom to make the battery/tape switch. I was horrified to see that the cubicle walls in the squat-style toilet came up only to my waist. Having no alternative, I hunkered down and began swapping the tape, only to hear the boss I was meeting enter the toilet himself, to use the urinal. All I could do was make the appropriate noises until he left, after what seemed like an eternity.

These days, of course, the technology has improved immeasurably: memory cards capable of recording hours of footage; miniature recording units; and high-quality lenses that can be concealed in a multitude of ways, either on the body or in external items like notebooks, pens, cigarette packages and bags.

These technological advances have led to a proliferation of relatively cheap 'spy cameras' available online or in gadget shops. EIA steers clear of such low-end devices, which are targeted more at hobbyists and have a high failure rate. It does not make sense to spend months preparing for a mission, and money on airfares and hotels, only to be let down by cheap kit.

Instead EIA sources its covert equipment from specialist or bespoke providers, such as those who supply television companies or government enforcement agencies. Thanks to investing in more high-end gear, EIA has had a very low kit-failure rate. It has been money well spent on avoiding one of an investigator's worst nightmares: the loss of irreplaceable visual evidence.

As well as reliability, EIA seeks robustness in its equipment. Investigations often take place in remote locations with no access to technical back-up should any component break. Another important factor when choosing kit is plausibility. Years ago I tested some of the first camera glasses. Although the idea of recording whatever I looked at was appealing, the fact that the glasses had thick black rims, and required a lead that ran down my back to a bulky recording unit, made the set-up totally impractical. Likewise a company recently offered EIA a camera concealed in a plastic water-bottle. Fine if you control the place where the meeting will be held; not so good if you are doing an investigation overseas and cannot carry liquids on to aircraft. Even if you could, it would be strange to turn up for an undercover meeting in a place like Vietnam clutching a half-full water bottle with an English label.

Despite technological advances, the fundamental importance of thorough preparation before embarking on undercover filming remains the same. While the right kit is important, being able to get into the right situation, and to get out safely, is paramount. Central to this is the creation of a credible cover story, or 'legend'. In EIA's work there are broadly two types of undercover filming situations, which can be described as observational or interactive.

The first kind involves documentation of a location where open filming is not possible. Examples of such situations include wildlife markets and sensitive areas like border crossings or ports. For market surveys, the aim is to find out what illegal wildlife products are on sale, and their sources and prices. Open filming in such situations would arouse suspicion and limit the possibility of talking to the sellers. Although this is fairly low risk, it is important that the person doing the undercover filming blends in. For instance it would be strange if a white person was wandering around a market off the tourist trail, asking the price of tiger bones.

The interactive work requires a more detailed set-up and is potentially higher risk. In essence it involves the investigator posing as a dealer or buyer and meeting with targets believed to be involved in the illegal trade of timber or wildlife. The aim is to engage the target in conversation about the contraband being offered and how the business works, such as source countries, smuggling methods and which officials are bribed. This is done by the investigator convincing the target that he or she is a plausible buyer, for which a detailed cover story is needed, involving props like a fake business card and website connected to a dummy company.

Such meetings usually take place at the target's business premises or sometimes nearby hotels rather than at a location where the investigator is in control and can set up the hidden kit in advance. This means that the investigator must react quickly upon being shown into the meeting room, to ensure that the target is in shot during the entire conversation. Security is obviously an important consideration in such circumstances. EIA undercover operatives always work in teams of two and prepare in advance for the meeting.

When working on a major illegal logging case in Indonesia I was in contact with a timber broker in Jakarta who asked to meet at my hotel. Of course I did not want him to come to the place I was staying, because of security and also because I wanted to pass myself off as a wealthy trader, which would have been unbelievable in my modest hotel. So before agreeing to the meeting I surveyed five-star hotels in Jakarta, to find one with the right combination of opulence and low security at the entrance, meaning that the covert kit that was in a bag would not be discovered.

The final piece of advice is to think carefully about why undercover filming is to be used in a certain situation. It is a technique that should be reserved only for situations where open filming is not possible, and should not become routine.

Used correctly it can lead to the production of powerful and effective films. The example from Jakarta described above was part of an exhaustive EIA investigation into a major timber smuggling syndicate spanning Indonesia, Singapore, Hong Kong and the mainland. It involved a series of undercover meetings, all caught on hidden camera. When the resulting film was released at a press conference in Jakarta it ran on national television stations for days, prompting the office of the Indonesian President to request a copy. He then launched an unprecedented crackdown, which marked a vital turning point in the country's struggle against illegal logging.

www.eia-international.org

Nigel Butcher
Technical Development Officer
Royal Society for the Protection of Birds (RSPB)

I took on the role of Technical Development Officer for the RSPB after seeing it advertised in the *Cambridge Evening News*. One of the bullet points in the advert asked for a background in electronics, and, having studied electronic engineering – and with an interest in birds – I found the job that I have enjoyed since the year 2000.

My role is to provide technical and electronic support to the Conservation Science department. The remit of the role is not confined to working for that team only; support is given to the Species Protection team as well as to the entire RSPB reserve network. Here's a brief overview of some of the electronic equipment the RSPB uses in its conservation work.

Equipment for conservation

Temperature data loggers have been used since the '90s for determining incubation behaviour and the success or otherwise of active nests. They are small coin-sized devices that can be used to autonomously record temperature over a defined period of time. The digital data can be retrieved, viewed and

evaluated after it has been recorded. The sensor is inserted into the nest cup and indicates at what points during the day a bird was off the nest; it can also show if, and when, the nest happens to fail, owing to predation for example. When a brooding bird is on the nest the temperature remains fairly constant; when it leaves, the temperature fluctuates according to the weather. This could be useful for film crews to learn the normal behaviour at a nest before installing cameras.

Nest cameras have been developed over the years as an extension to the data logger to determine the reason for nest failure and the identity of any predators.

Cine cameras and time lapse recorders were all part of the early conservationists' armoury. Digital recording systems have been in use since their introduction in 2004. Miniature cameras consuming power as low as 20mA can be used for purely research applications as well as for film-making. The RSPB started using infra-red light at this time for filming the Montserrat oriole in low-light situations. The need for invisible 940nm (wavelength) light was evident in such a deep afforested location. Lower wavelengths are much more suited to film-making, however, as cameras are more sensitive to 850nm light; yet this wavelength of light emits a visible red glow which may cause disturbance or make the nest more obvious to predators. To reduce the potential impacts of this (and possible criminal activities by those who would steal eggs or chicks, or lay down poison, and may be alerted by a red glow) the RSPB now always uses 940nm equipment.

Thermal cameras are another tool available to conservationists: they can provide a nocturnal insight into behaviour without the need to flood the area with infra-red (or visible) light.

When filming in the field, camera size and particularly lens size can be a problem with certain bird species. An effort to camouflage the unit certainly helps, as does introducing dummy equipment (or the equipment itself) in advance. Raptors can see their reflection in the lens when cameras are sited at close quarters and in these situations a pinhole lens and bullet camera are better. Some species are very prone to nest desertion, so extra care is taken when filming them, but there are also huge differences between individuals. One bird may be wary and another very accommodating, so don't just assume the best or worst! For protected species within the UK a species disturbance licence has to be obtained if disturbance is involved (such as by the placing of a recording

151

device in or near a nest) and if a camera is installed a photographic licence will be needed too.

The early digital recording systems used by RSPB had used sensors to wake and trigger the recording. With the advent of video motion detection, image capture at only key times (ie where the movement of an animal is detected) is possible. Active zones can be selected across your camera image, and small or significant pixel changes within these areas can initiate recording (using these zones can help to avoid recording unwanted images such as foliage waving in the wind). This can be useful for film-making as well as for research and it means the equipment can be left without an operator for days at a time, yet all of the best bouts of action are recorded. In recent times camcorders with large x70 optical zooms are used with external battery packs so that they can operate for 3–4 days unattended.

Location informs the decision as to whether an electronic monitoring/recording job is cabled or uses wireless transmission of some kind. Line-of-sight microwave transmission equipment is cheap but comes with power limitations on licence-free frequencies. Image quality is lost across both cabled and wireless options and the choice is often determined by the terrain; a hard-wired installation is likely to be more reliable if it's feasible. It is important to use old cable, as rodents are certainly more likely to chew new fresh-smelling wire. Mobile phone (GSM) transmission is another useful option and with the greater bandwidth of 3 and 4G, much higher-resolution data can be transmitted, to locations that aren't line-of-sight, for a limited financial outlay.

Trail cameras are extensively used nowadays to monitor animal activity and, with their high pixel count, can be of broadcast quality.

Sound is also important and a simple playback system built using MP3 player technology can be used in the wild either to attract or deter a certain species for 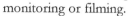 monitoring or filming.

In the same way that camera traps can be used to detect particularly nocturnal species, remote audio equipment can be programmed to come on at certain times to record the sound, so that the operator doesn't need to stay in the field. When the unit has been retrieved later, analysis software can help you look for the species of interest very quickly, and determine when they are most active and vocal.

Radio transmitters have been used in conservation for more than fifty years to locate and monitor movements of all kinds of animals. Transmitter tags which produce a radio signal begin at less than 0.2g and have been used on bees and dragonflies, but at these tiny weights life and range are very limited. The location of the animal is determined by researchers using receivers with antennas, and a number of points allow triangulation to reveal the position of the subject. Data logging units, which can record whenever a radio signal is detected, can be left out in the field to determine presence or absence of a particular animal.

Satellite tags are currently being produced with weights as low as 5g. These tags transmit their identification to an orbiting satellite owned by ARGOS which works out location by Doppler (time) shift. The more times the signal is received via triangulation the more accurate the estimate becomes. In the best cases you can locate the position of the tag to within 100m, but errors can be up to several kms. These tags are very expensive and the data costs can be too. Heavier satellite tags can combine GPS receivers that then transmit this location – this provides information accurate to under 10m. Many other tags incorporating GPS are available to track wildlife, but these can require re-catching the animal to download the data, or short-range wireless download which, of course, limits the range. More and more equipment incorporates cellular connectivity for data transfer. Tracking devices can use this as well as any remote data collection system.

Unmanned Aerial Vehicles (UAVs) can be used to monitor wildlife and, with cameras such as GoPros on board, can provide excellent habitat information. Legal flying heights have to be adhered to; in the UK this is 400 ft (approx 120m). Other equipment such as thermal cameras or camcorders can be flown – the size and payload of the frame will determine what can be carried. Radio tracking with UAVs can be beneficial, as the extra height allows birds to be detected at greater distance.

Developments are ongoing with battery capacities – particularly with Lithium cells, which are improving all the time. Much of this is driven by the mobile electronics market, and while hunger still remains for this technology further gains will be made. Miniature solar cell efficiency is coming on in leaps and bounds and where remote power is required this will be extremely useful. Additionally, further investment even in some of the less wealthy nations means that mobile phone and internet connectivity will aid conservation further.

www.rspb.org.uk

Madelaine Westwood
Founder and Director
Great Apes Film Initiative (GAFI)

I love films. They move us, inspire us, make us laugh and call us to action. As human beings we are genetically programmed to respond to images, music and sounds because they reach parts of our consciousness beyond the thinking brain. It is this extraordinary relationship between film and humans that makes film-making one of the most powerful conservation tools that we possess, and it is probably why I have worked in wildlife and conservation film-making for over twenty years.

In 2005 I was asked to go to Indonesia to make a film about the inter-relationship of birds, the forest and the people. It was quite a challenge, as the location was notoriously difficult to access. My guide Panut and I travelled for two days by motorbike and canoe to get to the location in the forest – but we couldn't find it. The GPS co-ordinates told me where it should be but instead I found scorched, smouldering stumps. The birds were gone, the trees were gone and the people were gone – victims of the ravenous palm oil industry.

Devastated, there was nothing we could do but turn back; but returning along the rutted earth track on the motorbike we suddenly skidded to a halt. High above, in a wooden hut on stilts, a man was pointing a gun at us. Panut dismounted and bravely went across to speak to him, managing to convince the man that we were bird watchers. The hunter invited us to listen to his bird impressions – and they were excellent. It transpired that he used them to attract birds from the forest,

154

catching and selling his bounty to the international wild bird trade. The hunter was also looking for a buyer for the skins of a tigress and her two cubs that he had killed a few days beforehand. Our 'host' informed us that the forest was abundant in wildlife and therefore he could take what he liked. I honestly find it difficult to describe my reaction; I was containing rage at the loss of such precious, highly-endangered animals; fear choked me, as the hunter had nothing to lose by killing us; and I felt an overwhelming sense of futility: what on earth could I do to stop this?

As I left Indonesia I knew I had to do something – but what? I am not wealthy, powerful, influential and I don't have a relevant PhD – but somehow I had to reach the people who were responsible for poaching, illegal logging, bushmeat, devastation caused by the palm oil industry etc. I didn't have much to offer, but I work in the most powerful communications industry we have. Surely we could do something together.

For many years I had heard film-makers say that their films needed to be seen by the people who lived and worked alongside the environmental issues facing our planet, so this is where I would start – but I needed help. First I headed for the conservationists – the first person I hooked up with on this new mission was Ian Redmond (Great Apes Survival Partnership (GRASP)) who advised me to restrict my actions to one highly-endangered species and then, when I knew what I was doing, I would be able to offer a template of the methods developed to other organisations and film-makers working on behalf of other species and habitats.

So now I just needed the right films to show. I went to influential broadcast partners in wildlife film-making: Brian Leith worked at Granada Wild and was on the board of Filmmakers For Conservation, and Neil Nightingale was Head of the Natural History Unit at the BBC. Both men worked hard to get me fifteen films that I could license for conservation and education use without charge. Together we had created the Great Apes Film Initiative (GAFI), and the films were sent out to do their job. They went to presidents and government ministers to lobby for law enforcement and environmental protection; they were aired on national television in five African countries to reach a mass audience; and they were distributed to be shown to local communities in schools, karaoke bars or riverboats. Wherever people gathered we screened films through our 'on the ground' NGO partners.

It hasn't always been always easy as we have to reach our audience, and much of it lives in remote areas; so wading through rivers and clambering up mountainsides is a frequent challenge. When we arrive, facilities are often minimal: the venues range from mud huts with holes in the roofs to brick churches where we find ingenious ways to exclude daylight from the gaping holes they use as windows. We rarely have electricity, and carrying the heavy generators requires the team to be fit. One element that is always abundant is the viewers; children and their parents have been known to walk for miles to attend the first screening of their lives.

In Uganda in 2008 we had a screening in association with the Gorilla Organisation and nearly one thousand children arrived, many of whom had walked for up to twenty miles to be there. Unfortunately the venue, a local church, was no longer available – the priest had changed his mind. I respect his decision but it left us with a huge problem. We had to set up in a tiny schoolroom, and repeatedly showed the film to as many people as we could fit in, but hundreds of children had to walk all that way home without seeing the films. We were devastated for the children and vowed to create something that did not depend on a location and could transcend logistical constraints. It took two years to develop, but -- with help from the Ape Alliance, James Belcher and Electric Pedals -- the answer is an entertaining, sustainable way of screening films: a pedal-powered cinema (involving a stationary bicycle pedalled to power the cinema via a dynamo) specially created to be robust enough for the demands of the field. The first people to receive it were the same children in Uganda who had walked all that way to the unsuccessful screening two years previously, and they couldn't wait to get their hands on it.

In the last ten years since GAFI was created over 300 million people have seen our films and, thanks to our sixty-eight NGO partners, the results of our screenings are evident. Together we have set up wildlife clubs, planted thousands of trees, educated an army, plantation workers, organic farmers, wildlife management trainees, school and university students and many national park rangers, supported school visits to their forested areas, and delivered nine pedal-powered cinemas to sanctuaries and partners.

These statistics are wonderful but, for me, GAFI's work is summed up by the story of a woman who attended a screening in a Ugandan forest. This had previously been her home before the national park had been created to protect mountain gorillas, with the result that her family -- along with many others --

was removed. It was obviously an emotional occasion for her and she stood quietly at the back of the room suckling a tiny baby in her arms. On the screen came images of a gorilla mother. also suckling her tiny baby: the look of shock on the woman's face was clear. After the film she spoke to our educator, telling him that she did not know that gorilla mothers were the same as human mothers: she was going home to tell her husband that he could no longer illegally take wood from the forest because it was the home of 'her sister'. That is the power of film.

GAFI believes that every single person has skills and abilities that can help; they may not be directly in film-making but they can contribute to a film's success. This means that every person has the capability to make a difference; you just have to use what you have got. I am certainly grateful to the two people who made me use what I have got: the hunter and the priest.

www.gafi4apes.org

Neil Grubb
Amateur Film-maker
Oasis – The Birds of the Esk Valleys

I have been an amateur maker of wildlife films since 2006. At the time of writing I have made four, each of which took two years to produce. My films are made for the general public, to show wildlife in its local environment and to educate and entertain. I have shown these films to many local and national clubs and societies, including at RSPB and Scottish Ornithologists' Club meetings. Documentary-making is an enjoyable challenge and has afforded me a much greater appreciation of the work of the professionals. I hope this case study will show that, with limited resources, an amateur can produce films that make a difference by showcasing local wildlife and promoting environmental awareness.

157

My home is Roslin Glen, a haven for wildlife and part of the Esk Valley river system, which forms a green corridor through Midlothian in southeast Scotland. I had used a long-standing interest in photography to document local wildlife, and began film-making when a friend lent me a standard definition camcorder. The plan was to document one of the first recorded breedings of the Eurasian nuthatch in the Lothian Region, but I became interested in using video to tell a story. The first sequences I shot were uninteresting and did not flow well, and I quickly learned that I needed to record close-up and wide shots, establishing shots and cutaways. Editing was done using Windows Movie Maker, which was ideal as it was simple for an untutored beginner to use. The end result was a twenty-minute film, *Northern Frontier*, which, despite its rough quality, was well received by my local branch of the Scottish Ornithologists' Club. Two hundred DVD copies were requested, for distribution as a supplement to the annual Lothian Bird Report.

I wanted to learn more about film-making, and to make better films. Although much could be learned from books and online, networking with local contacts was the best way to improve my skills. A good decision was to join a local film-making club, the Edinburgh Cine and Video Society. There were no wildlife film-makers at the weekly meetings but I learned much from members' experience of documentary making, specifically about production planning, audio recording, editing, narration and music copyright. I also made contact with a composer and pianist, Dmytro Morykit, who eventually produced the music for *Oasis* and its sequel, *Outlands*. The second, equally important, aspect to networking was to make best use of friends and contacts in the local birdwatching community. This gave me very useful information about the locations of several breeding species and saved considerable time scouting out subjects for the film. Internet forums such as the Digital Video Information Network (www.dvinfo.net) and Indietalk (www.indietalk.com) provided very helpful lessons on equipment, editing and project planning.

After making a second, short film about breeding peregrines, filmed by digiscoping (using a digital camera with a birding telescope) with a Canon Ixus compact digital camera, I began the project that eventually became *Oasis*. The plan was to make a better quality film that would take the viewer on a journey up the Esk Valleys to see the less well-known bird-life, which the casual observer would be likely to overlook. I wanted to record behaviour, songs and calls of several local bird species, and to show the diverse habitats within and near the valley. I purchased some better equipment – a Canon XL-H1A HDV camera, a Manfrotto tripod with a fluid video head, a Zoom H4 digital audio recorder (second-hand from a local music shop) and a Sennheiser shotgun microphone. The advantage of the HDV camera was that it could be adapted to use my Canon SLR camera lenses, giving a very high magnification factor.

The documentary begins with a description of the Esk Valley, with visuals of winter flocks (waxwings, starlings and finches). Further up the valley, in a steep gorge, ravens and peregrines are encountered – and revisited later on. Waterside birds such as kingfishers and dippers have made a remarkable recovery as water quality has improved. Other woodland species such as tawny owls, woodpeckers, redstarts and nuthatches are studied. *Oasis* closes by observing some of the passerines of the upland Esk watershed such as whinchats, redpolls and grasshopper warblers.

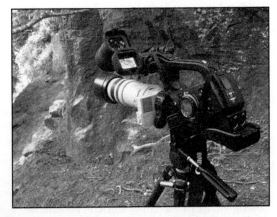

The first stage was to plan the key elements of the film. Knowledge of regular breeding sites for several species – peregrine, raven, nuthatch, spotted flycatcher and whinchat – provided components that would anchor the film. I planned trips throughout the breeding season to film these birds. While filming these I took advantage of incidental finds such as an irruption of waxwings, a particularly confiding grasshopper warbler, and a green woodpecker which photobombed while I was filming ravens! The crucial element was time – in the end it took two years to acquire the fifty hours of video from which *Oasis* was distilled.

The second stage was filming and cataloguing of clips – having used HDV format, I had to transfer all clips from tape to PC. Tapes were indexed in a Word document to log their content, quality, and other details such as close or wide shot, and lighting conditions. My video-editing package, Adobe Premiere Pro 5, did allow indexing to be accomplished digitally, but I preferred to use a simple paper index. As well as the planned and opportunistic shots of the bird subjects, I took time at each site to acquire plenty of shots of the habitat and of related plants, wild flowers and non-avian wildlife. These could later be used as establishing shots, cutaways and closing shots for each of the sections of *Oasis*.

Having this combination of planned and unplanned shots altered the narrative thread that was to run through the film. This had the advantage of adding variety to it but did complicate the editing process. It took several weeks to assemble the key clips in approximate order and trimmed roughly to length to produce an initial vision of what *Oasis* would eventually look like. At this stage no audio or video transitions, audio level editing, colour grading, captions or graphics were included.

Writing a narration script was a new experience and it required many drafts, each read out aloud as the video played, before settling on a final version. I took a while to realise that less is more in narration, and I learned several lessons at this stage: short, simple sentences work best; narration should complement the video and not overwhelm it; there is no value describing something that is obvious to the viewer; and the best narration informs without being obtrusive. I found this a difficult balance to achieve. Narration was recorded using the Zoom recorder – while I am quite accustomed to talking in front of large student audiences through my work, it was much more difficult to read the narration script aloud perfectly, using appropriate and not exaggerated intonation. It was easiest to divide the script into small chunks and record each separately – even then it sometimes took seven or eight attempts to get it right.

After recording the narration, I took the shot sequences through several iterations of editing, building video transitions but eventually removing all of them except the simplest straight cuts and fades to black at the end of sections. Complex transitions are distracting and I simplified this aspect of *Oasis* with each edit. Audio levels and noise levels were different among batches of clips and it took considerable time to make these consistent by level adjustment and noise filtering. Simple introductory titling and rolling credits worked best at each end of the film. For audio, unwanted sounds (eg people talking, cars, planes, dogs barking) were edited out and additional ambient sound added using samples recorded in the field using the Zoom recorder for that purpose.

Working with Dmytro Morykit on music was one of the most inspiring aspects of the making of *Oasis*. It was done on a fee basis, but we have become friends and collaborators. I transferred an edited and narrated draft on to a tablet, and met Dmytro with ideas about the mood and pace to be conveyed by music in the different sections of the film. He improvised several musical themes to fit the different sections of the film, and then we set to record his performance. I used both the Zoom recorder and the onboard camera microphone, and found that the best sound was recorded pointing the mics behind the piano – otherwise the clack of fingernails on keys, and thud of feet on pedals, were recorded with disproportionate intensity! There are other options for music for amateur film-makers on a limited budget; royalty-free music recordings can be used, but such off-the-shelf music may not quite fit the mood the film is trying to convey. Also, there are many musicians out there who can be contacted via internet forums who might welcome the chance to collaborate on a no-fee or minimal-fee basis as a first step.

The final stage was bringing video, natural audio, narration and music together. This was much more difficult than I imagined and I spent a month sorting out audio levels so that the natural sounds, music and voice worked in balance. Also, the length of many of the video sequences had to be shortened or extended slightly to allow for the length of the narration and music segments. I spent so much time on editing that I eventually had to say "Stop – this is good enough, and the best you can do with the limited quality of the material you have". You can watch *Oasis* at https://vimeo.com/27411516.

Since making *Oasis*, I have produced a sequel film called *Outlands – Wild Places of the Lothians*. With each film I try to do better with video, audio, narration and editing quality! This film is now doing the rounds of local and national clubs and societies and it gives me great satisfaction using my work to show the public local wildlife. Documentary making is a very enjoyable challenge and I now have a much greater appreciation of the work of the professionals.

In presenting *Oasis* and *Outlands*, with accompanying talks, I have been able to show people what is out there in nature, if only they take time to look. My films have been used as a method to raise awareness of the precarious nature of the habitats shown, and the importance of preserving them. By word of mouth, my talks and film showings have increased (and recently doubled) attendances at meetings of the Scottish Wildlife Trust branch, and Roslin Heritage Society. Through these meetings *Oasis* has

161

drawn attention to local housing development applications and both wind farm and open-cast mine proposals, thus stimulating many locals to involve themselves in environmental concerns.

https://vimeo.com/channels/roslinnature

Rob Spray
Diver, Photographer, Film-maker
Seasearch East

Seasearch East is the East Anglian outpost of the Marine Conservation Society's national underwater wildlife recording project, run by Dawn Watson and Rob Spray. Their dive surveys have put the marine flora and fauna of the southern North Sea on the map, using images from an environment too often regarded as a stormy, barren wilderness. Their headline story has been the revelation of North Norfolk's chalk reef, stretching twenty miles across the top of the county and, off Cromer, reaching a width of three miles. It's a vibrant refuge for hundreds of species and has become a standard bearer for this heavily exploited sea.

Issues close to home tend to be overlooked; bringing wildlife to wider attention ignites a debate about what people are willing to threaten or knowingly ignore. This is clearly the case with marine life, which also suffers from 'celebrity holiday' syndrome where the 'good stuff' seen on television is almost always abroad, presented by a gurning household name. This presents a challenge: to surprise a blasé public with amazing wildlife from beneath their very own, doggy-paddling feet.

When we started to explore the North Norfolk chalk reef we didn't know its extent, visual appeal or biodiversity. When we started to dive it speculatively – using offshore shadows on Google Earth as initial survey sites – we were simply recording for Seasearch. In fact the chalk just went on, and by the end of the diving season we had found the longest chalk reef in Europe.

The sharing of some still photographs gained national exposure for the reef, but only as a 'believe-it-or-not' novelty. However, those first portraits of animals on the reef led to a demand for more and we realised that further coverage could add to the story: photography and video are perceived in different ways. People are impressed but not entirely convinced by polished, portrait close-ups. When set in seascapes film can carry a lot more weight in conveying the habitat that exists. Our emphasis moved on to provide this contextual coverage; first stills for the press until we caught the eye of some conservation educators and were encouraged to produce visitor centre films for the local Wildlife Trust.

The complications of filming are multiplied underwater; not to say it's easy elsewhere, just that working in a corrosive domain where humans can't breathe adds new difficulties! Our initial filming used a modest digital HD camcorder. That gave some decent results despite the limited control offered by our simple housing – little more than 'record' and 'zoom'. White balance was either 'set and regret' or determined at the whim of the camera's underwater setting. Success in either case was variable, as underwater scenery has a strong colour cast.

Things improved markedly with the advent of 'mirrorless' stills cameras. These were designed from the outset to properly support video shooting and gave better control in reasonably-priced compact housings. They offered a wide choice of good lenses too – which included video-friendly features like stepless aperture adjustment and fast, silent autofocus.

One saving grace for us is that the chalk of the reef is a pretty good white reference which baselines auto and manual adjustment when white balancing the camera. Much of the reef is shallow and quite bright, so additional lighting which one might otherwise use is impractical to restore 'normal' colour to large seascapes. 'White' underwater varies with direction, elevation, time, surface conditions, surroundings and probably twenty other things. Achieving acceptable white balance is the most persistent challenge: the strong casts underwater make it difficult to set correctly – the white balance can't be adjusted much before a channel saturates. Our current, non-video dedicated, mirrorless cameras don't offer high video recording rates. Those low bitrates ($<30Mb/s$) need to be fed clean, stable scenery with reasonable contrast to compress well. The particularly impressive in-body stabilisation on the systems we use helps save a lot of data, and, as ever, performance improves as camera technology develops.

Mirrorless cameras with exotic wide lenses and matching ports are a gift underwater as refraction reduces a typical '28mm' (75 degree) air view by about a quarter (through flat glass). With a fisheye lens and dome port we can film a near-180 degree field and get much closer to the subject. This reduces the amount of water in front of the subject, improving lighting and the quality of the resulting footage. At the other end of the scale we film animals *in situ* with macro lenses – this is physically tough as it's tricky remaining still in a surge or current. No species has been more of a challenge than the little cuttlefish (*Sepiola atlantica*) which is the size of a bumble bee and similarly flighty. Luckily the public is as unfamiliar with most marine life as it is with our favourites (such as this cuttlefish) so we don't have to rely on catching the impossible on film. When we do find the rarer ones you can bet we'll have the wrong lens on – and you can't change main lenses underwater. With the small size of mirrorless systems and their ports it can be feasible to use external 'wet' lenses for macro or wide-angle adaptation.

The increasing reputation of the reef has built media attention. In 2010 Norfolk Wildlife Trust asked us to help with a multiscreen show at the Forum in Norwich, which had the advantage of being downstairs from the local BBC documentary team. This was an opening for us, as was their use of an underwater film crew who talked the talk but didn't know the area (unlike us). Underwater filming is expensive and visiting crews can't spend the same time as locals on finding interesting  animals. Whatever the ability of the professionals, it is impossible to provide good conditions on tap – and even if you do, the use of presenters can eat up filming days. Our wildlife footage supported the presenter shots the BBC did manage to get. The resulting *Inside Out* special doubled their usual audience for that slot and won a local TV award.

Since that first co-operative effort between us and the BBC the scheme of supporting land-based presenters with our underwater footage has worked well. So far no one has quibbled over the technical quality of material – although there's such a 'race to the bottom' that it's a constant challenge to preserve quality when editors aren't familiar with formats. Some broadcasters will even send YouTube footage straight to air, assuming that's the best it can be. Our 30fps files have been ingested into editing programs at varying quality; nowadays we usually convert them ourselves to suit the situation.

During our media encounters we've become more practised in making the most of the limited material that even multiple dives on difficult sites can provide. The discovery of a bed of fallen prehistoric trees in 2014 was, we thought, interesting if esoteric. We were pleased when the local BBC team liked the look of the footage we had shot and put together a supporting documentary segment. This mode of operation allows short television programmes to be made without the expense of a professional dive team. In this case, once we knew the date of the broadcast, we briefed a press agency that the programme would be going out and told it the story behind it. That made the discovery of the 10,000 year-old trees into a news story with some cool pictures to support it and, in suitably circular fashion, once it was definitely going to be news, the BBC got more strongly behind it and wanted us on air during the day. That national coverage got way more viewers than the documentary; and the supporting clip was the most-played that day on the BBC website, garnering more than half a million views. The story spread to Indian websites, French educational magazines and eventually even the local paper!

None of this makes anyone rich, but now the subject has a momentum of its own, if we ever mention we're divers we're often told earnestly about the wonders of the local seabed. That's positive reinforcement: people actually want to know more about their local reef!

It's not hyperbole to suggest that the chalk reef might have passed under the radar of the Marine Conservation Zone (MCZ) process had it not been for the public awareness raised by the footage from the seabed. Backing this up with methodical wildlife surveys has made the case for designating the reef as a protected area irrefutable by any standard. Whether the implementation of the MCZ lives up to the needs of the reef's wildlife remains to be seen; conservation has been a low priority under the current administration but we won't let up the pressure on them!

www.1townhouses.co.uk   www.youtube.com/user/reallymadrob

Abbie Barnes
Film-maker, Presenter, Conservationist
Song Thrush Productions

Many man-made environmental issues, if not all, appear fearfully overwhelming at first glance, and it's this intimidation factor that can initiate the fight-or-flight response – to ignore the issue, or actively to take up the challenge of mitigating it. Six years ago, thirteen year-old me decided I couldn't just sit around and do nothing about rapacious worldwide destruction, so I took up my camcorder and began to make films in order to make a difference and share my messages. Since then, I have spoken in the European Parliament, helped initiate World Orangutan Day, been awarded nationally and internationally, spoken to school groups and societies across the UK, climbed the highest free-standing mountain in the world to document the loss of its glaciers, filmed with the United Nations to promote World Environment Day and World Ocean Day 2015, and more.

Through my work I aim to educate – to offer facts and figures – and to provide positive, practical solutions to whatever issue is in focus. I aim to install in my viewers and audiences the belief that every action counts; that we should all be taking full responsibility, and acting now, in order to secure a sustainable future.

Whether you want simply to express your opinion, or to begin an international movement, film can be a powerful way to capture attention and get your message across. You need to consider who your target audience is; for children, think about making an animated and fun-filled film, perhaps with a song they will remember. For an older audience, be sure to utilise their focus to get as much key information across as possible, without overloading them – there is a fine balance. Think outside the box. You don't have to stick with a factual documentary-style film; experiment with role-play, comedy, or musicals.

When you know what style of film you want to produce, you need to research your subject. Speak to people from both sides of the debate, learn the true facts and figures, even go and witness the issue first-hand in order to gain a deep level of understanding.

Once you have made your film you need to get it on to people's screens. In my experience the number one way to achieve this is through the use of social media. This takes time and dedication, but you should be used to that by now, having just produced your own film! By uploading your film to a major video-hosting site, such as YouTube or Vimeo, you make it easy for people to access, and even easier to share online.

I have been fortunate enough to have built a decent number of followers on social media, leading to an ever-rising number of views of my videos. I produced my first conservation film *Save Our Oceans, Recycle Your Plastic* with a film festival competition in mind, so I stuck strictly to their guidelines of three minutes total length for the film. Sometimes short really is sweet, as I won the competition, receiving my award from Sir David Attenborough. The experience proved to me that it only takes one or two films to capture people's attention, and you are off!

Perhaps the most difficult thing to achieve with conservation film-making, but definitely the most important, is your message really touching the heart of your viewers and making them want to act. In my opinion there is no point in making a film that brushes over the subject, allowing viewers to move on and forget everything they have just experienced. You need to engage with them: aim to inspire and motivate. Ensure that you choose a subject that touches your own heart, and this process should be easy.

So there you have it, your first conservation film. Well done! Remember to reflect on why you made that film. It's easy to move on feeling proud and accomplished, but your work is never truly complete until that conservation issue is solved. After all, film is merely a medium to raise awareness: but do it right, and you may contribute to resolving the issue.

www.songthrushproductions.co.uk

Mike Pandey
Environmentalist and Wildlife Conservation Film-maker
Riverbank Studios, New Delhi, India

Conservation films … agents of change

Can a film make a 'real' difference?

'Conservation' and 'sustainability' are words we have all heard and been familiar with for decades, but those years have seen very little change at ground level. Good intentions and legislation alone cannot transform our world; it's only when people change, and lifestyles change, that we shall be able to make a difference.

It was heartening to hear Sir David Attenborough speak, in one of his latest films, of conservation and the need for protection of the earth's natural resources. Our world is going through a crisis, and there is an urgent need for a global conservation movement. Natural resources are depleting at an alarming rate, which the earth is unable to keep pace with. Whether it is air, water, health of the soil, or in fact the survival of all life forms: all is at stake today.

I believe that films can be powerful and effective tools for generating awareness, and in the shortest time possible. Powerful films that speak the truth. Making conservation films – in comparison to other films – may be difficult and challenging, and may at times seem impossible, but persistence and perseverance are key. There are many examples, around the world, of films that have made a difference and become agents of change.

My film, *Shores of Silence: Whale Sharks in India* – a Wildscreen Panda award-winner – is considered a hard-hitting conservation film and, to quote a UN spokesman, 'a film that helped to save a species from extinction'. The film helped bring legislative changes not only in India but internationally. But the journey was rough, and came with a bundle of problems: funding aside, there was a number of other obstacles in our path.

I first saw the whale shark when travelling from the East African coast to India. On the second day we spotted a group of seven whale sharks swimming at a little distance from our ship. They kept pace and followed us for eight days, until we lost sight of them as we approached the Indian coast. Years later, spotting the decomposing carcass of a whale shark on a beach, I was informed that it was a 'garbage fish' not consumed in India; only its liver was useful, and was used to make boot polish and waterproofing material for boats by some fishing communities. It was shocking to hear that the largest fish in the world was being wasted in this way. All my protests with the authorities fell on deaf ears; no one else believed that the Indian coastline was frequented by whale sharks. I was told what I had seen was just the carcass of a dead fish that had drifted from somewhere else and washed ashore, but it had certainly been a whale shark.

"We don't have a history of whale sharks, so how can we kill something that does not exist in our waters?" a senior officer enquired. Even the internet did not show India as a possible whale shark destination. I started looking for sponsors and funding agencies: international broadcasters; TV networks; even my friends from the media. There were no takers: all were reluctant to fund a story that they believed contained no truth.

According to global statistics at that time, the highest numbers of whale sharks were in the Ningaloo marine park in Western Australia, followed by the Gulf of Mexico and Honduras, and a few odd ones in Thailand, Western Africa and Chinese seas. The IUCN Red List showed the whale shark's status as indeterminate. The whale shark had remained invisible in Indian waters and even globally; it was not protected, nor even declared endangered. We spent almost two years looking for them in Indian waters, visiting fishing villages, searching over 8,000 km of coastline to find a creature no one believed existed there.

We finally found them on the western coast of India near a small fishing village. The fishermen did not even have a name for whale sharks. They just called it 'the barrel fish', because they were using empty barrels, attached with ropes to hooks, to capture the giants. Many fishermen had lost their lives while capturing the whale sharks.

Meanwhile, as we were preparing to film, we heard of a businessman who had suddenly appeared in the area and was buying whale shark meat to make chicken-feed and rose manure. We discovered that this was just a front, and that he was actually exporting the meat to South East Asian countries, where it was considered a delicacy. The killing of whale sharks escalated owing to the sudden demand from this exporter.

Unknown to the world, nearly 1,200 whale sharks were being slaughtered on the western coast of India. A film *had* to be made to stop this senseless slaughter of the world's largest fish, a crucial link in the marine food chain. Making the film was one of my toughest challenges as a film-maker – we faced hostile fishermen, the invisible mafia and omnipresent administrative hurdles. It took over two years to complete.

When *Shores of Silence: Whale Sharks in India* was finally released, its first screening was held in Delhi, in the presence of government agencies, the WWF and wildlife NGOs. The audience and the press were shocked; a heavy silence prevailed. Finally came a question: "Is this India?" What followed made history. Government agencies decided to take immediate action to protect the species in Indian waters and the Arabian Sea.

Legislation usually takes decades, and several rounds of meetings and processes. But within three months of the film's release, the whale shark was brought under the protection of The Indian Wildlife Protection Act, 1972, bringing it into line with the tiger and the rhino. Anybody found killing a whale shark would now face seven years in prison and a heavy fine. This was the first time a marine species was achieved protection under law in Indian waters. The film had succeeded in making a difference.

The whale shark is a global heritage species, a migratory creature which follows warm currents around the globe. The increase in its slaughter on the Indian coast had led to a reduction in numbers spotted in the Philippines, Thailand, Malaysia and Australia. Many whale sharks migrating from Australia, to avoid the harsh winter, had become victims of this senseless killing. Their numbers were under severe threat worldwide. More had to be done.

We took the film to CITES (the Convention on International Trade in Endangered Species of Wild Fauna and Flora) in Santiago, Chile, and appealed for the whale shark's protection. While Britain secured protection for the basking shark, the whale shark got just a few votes. It was disappointing to see that members of the global community were not even aware of the presence of the whale shark around the Indian coastline. We lost the vote.

Hours later, heavy-hearted but undeterred, we decided to distribute thirty copies of the film to the delegates throughout the three days. On the third day, as the conference was closing down, the chairman asked for any unfinished business, and we immediately appealed for a re-vote. An overwhelming majority of hands rose up in favour of global protection for the whale shark. It prompted the chairman to ask the reason for the sudden change of minds. A delegate from the Philippines informed him that they had seen visuals which were "not only shocking, but frightening", and if the whale shark was not protected "today and now" it could become extinct within five years. Lost forever. The whale shark was granted global protection by CITES. It was put in Appendix 2, Schedule 2 of the global Wildlife Protection List.

A film had succeeded in making a difference globally, literally saving a species from extinction. It proved itself an effective tool of communication, education and awareness-generation. I feel there's a need for more such films. I have nothing against blue-chip films: they are important, entertaining and beautifully shot. But, until recently, most had a knack of avoiding the issues that threaten wildlife today, the reality of the threat of extinction every species faces. There is a need to make their watchers aware that the wonders of nature that they are witnessing are under a great threat. Hundreds of species are being lost every day due to the development and expansion that we call progress. But progress has a price. Life on earth is an interconnected and interdependent, fragile web, where each link is dependent on the others for survival. Our own survival on this planet is dependent on insects that pollinate our food and provide us with sustenance; on forests that provide us with water and air. Mankind cannot live in isolation. The need is to preserve an equilibrium, a balance, a harmonious ecosystem that has sustained life on this planet for millions of years. Its fragmentation could lead to the extinction of all life-forms on the planet, including mankind. Films can speak the truth, and the time is now.

To quote the late film-maker Nick Gordon, "*Shores of Silence* is a powerful conservation film, hard-hitting, and it tells us what we are doing to the planet. I use it wherever I go. It has made a global difference. It has actually saved a species on the brink of extinction from sliding away forever."

Similarly, my other films, *Vanishing Vultures* and *Vanishing Giants: Elephants* were about endangered species and the crises they were in. Over 79 million vultures, which constituted 99.9% of India's vulture population, had died due to the use of Diclofenac, a painkiller used by vets to treat livestock which proved lethal to the birds. The Prime Minister of India gave a directive to phase out the drug within six months. Two years later, however, the drug was still available and being used. The vulture population was in a tailspin towards extinction.

We decided to bring the issue into the public domain. The film, translated into local languages, reached millions of farmers across India via the public broadcasting system; once they discovered that the drug they were using was

171

killing the vultures, they destroyed all their stocks of Diclofenac. *Vanishing Vultures* was a hard-hitting film that worked from the grassroots upwards to the top; the policy-makers and the young. The film led to a Parliamentary debate, and within three weeks the drug-controller general was pressured into banning the production, manufacture and distribution of Diclofenac across India. The film also led to the setting-up of breeding centres for vultures, giving the critically-endangered scavenger a fighting chance for survival. The vulture is limping back, albeit slowly. A slow breeder, vultures lay only one egg a year. It will take over a hundred years for their population to stabilise.

I feel that one of the factors that led to the success of these films was that they weren't judgmental or didactic, or mere 'doom and gloom' stories. They touched the hearts and minds of people with the simple sharing of information. They made the audience aware of the issues, and how our own lives were connected to them, and also of the solutions that could help reverse the situation, and what each one of us can do to make a difference.

Humankind is a very young species, still evolving, making mistakes and – let us hope – learning. We have to understand that we share the planet with many other species. If we are really serious about having a future, and a better world, we all need to contribute in our small ways. As film-makers, we have the greater responsibility of taking value-based information to the people, and making them understand the challenges that we face, and also the difference we can make just by a little change in our lifestyles.

Wildlife film-making is exciting, exacting and sometimes fraught with danger. There are stonewalls too, plus endless delays, denied permissions, and an almost constant lack of funds, especially for conservation films. But films like these need to be made if we want a future. Luck, too, plays an important part. I guess I have been lucky and in the right place at the right time.

The very survival of our planet is under threat. If we want a future, we need to see a change in the way we have been treating the earth and its resources. Information, awareness and education have to reach the millions of people, especially in the developing countries, where communities have no knowledge of the challenges we are facing.

There is a need to understand the limitations of the planet we call home. There is a need to change our lifestyles and insatiable greed for more. We all hold the potential to make a difference. A single atom holds the power of the universe inside it. You and I – and anyone – can be that atom.

www.riverbankstudios.com

Will Anderson
Keo Films
Hugh's Fish Fight, Save Our Seas

Will Anderson joined Keo Films in 1998, straight from university. He took the classic route of starting as a Researcher, then working his way up through Assistant Producer, Director, Series Producer and is now Creative Director of Documentaries. He was Series Producer and Director for both *Hugh's Fish Fight* and the follow-up series *Save Our Seas*, both broadcast on Channel 4.

The idea for *Hugh's Fish Fight* came about after a meeting between Channel 4 and Keo Films to discuss a new campaigning series based on a food issue that Hugh Fearnley-Whittingstall would present. Chef, broadcaster, and Director of Keo Films, Hugh is well-known for his numerous *River Cottage* series, also shown on Channel 4. Initially the channel wanted to focus on some aspect of fisheries, but it wasn't until a further meeting with several marine conservation NGOs (including Greenpeace and the Marine Conservation Society) that the subject of discards was mentioned: half of the fish caught in the North Sea are thrown back, dead.

The 2010 series (three one-hour programmes, plus a fourth one later) became a multi-platform campaign that went on to attract over 870,000 supporters online, and received the support of Jamie Oliver, Stephen Fry, Coldplay, Richard Branson and other high-profile *fish fighters*, collecting a BAFTA along the way. A website was built and set up very quickly to start collecting signatures from people who wanted to see an end to the scandal of discarding fish at sea. It was phenomenally successful, winning many awards including a Broadcast Digital award. It was the first truly multi-platform campaign that brought together television and the internet in a unified response to a national problem. By the end of the third episode 500,000 people had signed the online petition against discards and the website had received twelve million page views.

Two years later the follow-up series *Save Our Seas* focused on creating Marine Conservation Zones in our seas, this time going global – to Antarctica, the Philippines and Thailand. Back in the UK, Hugh roused his army of Fish

Fighters to put pressure on supermarkets and the government to help Save Our Seas. The website, refreshed by Keo Digital, allowed members of the public to join Hugh's fish-fighting crew and e-mail the government expressing their concern about MCZs. Over the ad break of the last episode, Hugh asked people to tweet the major UK supermarkets to make sure their prawns were being fed on sustainable fishmeal. Over 16,000 people responded. This was the first time in the UK that Twitter had been used to gather public opinion and direct feedback in a campaign. As a result, a major Thai shrimp company has changed its practices regarding its prawnfeed supply. Live Twitter action during TV broadcasts is certainly something we shall see more of.

Three years after the original *Hugh's Fish Fight* series, Europe's politicians voted to ban discards (coming into effect from January 2016), the major supermarkets were persuaded to change their fish-sourcing policies, and many companies to change their tuna labelling. The series has been re-broadcast in twenty-eight other countries and gained 700,000 views on YouTube.

Hugh's Fish Fight is a hybrid in that it was commissioned by Channel 4 Features but obviously has a strong documentary element. Will Anderson believes the success was due to the clearly-defined hook: half of the fish caught in the North Sea are thrown back – what are we going to do about it? Added to that, Channel 4 also had the confidence that anything presented by Hugh Fearnley-Whittingstall would be popular with their audience.

Will's clear advice to anyone wanting to make films that make a difference is to Find The Story – that's the job of a film-maker – and not something that's necessarily obvious to conservation organisations. The story of *Hugh's Fish Fight* included Hugh's own journey and risk – initially no one knew how successful the campaign was going to be – which helped make viewers feel involved and want to keep watching. In particular Will also believes that the idea of waste (of discards) was a key attraction for viewers – people don't like waste. Once the hook is in place you can then unpack the rest of the story – rather than just presenting a flat issue from the start. This is a key reason why creative film-makers can help conservationists promote their issues.

Ten or more years ago it would have been very difficult to achieve the same success from a TV series. Back then viewers could have sent off for a fact-sheet at best, but these days the concept of two-screening (watching a TV show with your phone, pad or laptop by your side to help you find out more, or take action) has changed the possibilities and immediacy of action. It has enabled viewers to tell politicians and/or companies easily and quickly how much they care about an issue.

After the series, Keo was given some grants from charitable organisations in order to evaluate the success of the programmes. The first series had a follow-up fourth programme six months later, which Will believes was a strong tool in the campaign – letting people know that the issue wasn't going to go away – an incentive for those who were challenged to make changes.

www.fishfight.net   www.keofilms.com

Maarten van Rouveroy van Nieuwaal
Head of Video Production
Greenpeace International

Greenpeace's Modern Mind Bomb

To a great extent Greenpeace's campaigns are built on the power of the image. Pivotal to the work of the environmental organisation has always been the principle of 'bearing witness'. And central to that concept is the need to capture visual evidence of environmental crimes.

Shortly after Greenpeace got off the ground in the early seventies, Bob Hunter, one of the organisation's founding fathers, coined the term 'the mind bomb'. The idea – chronicled in the documentary *How to Change the World* – was to create an image with the power to resonate around the world, grab people's attention and inspire them into action.

One of Greenpeace's first expeditions provided a classic example of such a mind bomb. A harpoon fired from a Soviet whaler flew closely over the head of Greenpeace activists before exploding into the whale they were attempting to protect. The highly dramatic pictures were rushed back to shore and within hours flashed up on TV screens around the world. Global outrage over the brutal footage provided a huge boost to what was to become the Save the Whale campaign. A true 'viral' *avant la lettre*.

Screens and delivery platforms have changed, but the basic principles of that 'mind bomb' are still alive in the present day. Greenpeace's video productions

175

still consist of news and feature material, showcasing unseen and dramatic footage of environmental crimes. But short, creative productions for online distribution – produced in house, or in collaboration with freelance film-makers and creative agencies – have become an increasingly important part of the campaigns.

Powerful visuals, clarity of message and high production values are still important. But one element of the operation that has changed dramatically is distribution. Long gone are the days of television's monopoly on deciding what people watch. In the age of 'broadcast yourself', the possibilities for self-production and distribution are endless. But so too are the options for the viewer. To rise through the clutter of video content being uploaded to the internet requires much more than a strong message and high production values. Above all, your video needs measurable goals, a well-defined target audience and a strong distribution strategy to achieve results.

As an organisation with global reach yet finite resources, a key element to Greenpeace's operation has been its strategic choice of campaign targets. Obviously, worst offenders are most likely to bear the brunt of a campaign. Equally often, however, it is industry leaders or companies whose reputation is built on their positive public profile who can be pushed to drive real change.

Apple was such a Greenpeace target in the campaign to remove hazardous toxic materials from electronics, just as Lego was important in the push to save the Arctic, and Unilever (through its popular brands) proved pivotal in the effort to confront the palm oil industry.

Greenpeace's first viral video success came in 2009 with the so-called *Dove Onslaughter* production. The campaign, aimed against the destruction of the Indonesian rainforest, focused its effort on Unilever, which at the time was chairing the Round Table of Sustainable Palm Oil producers.

Parody and provocation have been the foundations of many online campaigns. *Dove Onslaughter* took a massively successful Ogilvy and Mather commercial for Dove (a brand owned by Unilever) and turned it against itself.

Dove's original *Onslaught* featured a young girl being bombarded by a rapid montage of aggressive marketing from the fashion and cosmetics industry. In Greenpeace's parody, a young Indonesian girl was confronted with a similarly fast-paced montage picturing the destruction of the rainforest that is required to make Dove's palm oil-containing products.

The video took off like a rocket, making it into viral video charts and bleeding into mainstream media such as the *Wall Street Journal* and Fox News. The millions of online and offline views prompted the Unilever board to sit up, take notice and review their role in decreasing the impact of the palm oil industry on Indonesia's rainforest.

Dove Onslaught (original)*:*
https://www.youtube.com/watch?v=Ei6JvK0W60I
Dove Onslaughter (Greenpeace parody)*:*
https://www.youtube.com/watch?v=odI7pQFyjso

Many similar campaigns followed in the wake of this success. Videos targeting Mattel (Barbie) and Nestlé (KitKat) further propelled progress on the campaign to stop the adverse impact of paper and palm oil industries in Indonesia. Productions aimed at Nike and Adidas helped drive these brands to remove toxic components from their clothing products.

Give the Orang Utan a Break (KitKat):
https://www.youtube.com/watch?v=VaJjPRwExO8

In recent times, Greenpeace has been turning up the heat on Shell in an effort to force the company away from its plans to drill for oil in the fragile Arctic. Here, too, being strategic and finding weak points in your opponent's armour has proven to be of critical importance. In this particular case, the campaign focused on the little-known relationship between Shell and one of its long-standing corporate partners, Lego.

Surfing a recent wave of interest in Lego, a Greenpeace video spoofing the massively-popular *Everything is Awesome* song, saw a miniature Lego Arctic engulfed by an oil spill caused by Shell. Owing in part to a clever seeding strategy, the video once again went viral and the pressure of millions of viewers, rising up in protest, forced Lego out of its long-standing partnership with Shell.

Everything Is Not Awesome (Lego):
https://www.youtube.com/watch?v=qhbliUq0_r4

Rarely will companies recognise publically that pressure from environmental groups has influenced their decisions. And attributing a campaign win to a single video will in most cases be a stretch. But the power of the mind bomb is undeniable, and viral video content is here to stay.

www.greenpeace.org/international

Rob Stewart
Film-maker
Sharkwater and *Revolution*

It started with *Sharkwater*. Initially working as a wildlife photographer, Toronto-born Rob Stewart turned to film-making as a more powerful way to change attitudes about sharks. He joined members of the Los Angeles-based Sea Shepherd Conservation Society aboard the *Ocean Warrior* for a four-month expedition to deter the poaching of sharks in Costa Rica and Ecuador, and started filming what became the multi-award winning 89-minute documentary *Sharkwater*.

In the movie Rob debunks historical stereotypes and media depictions of sharks as bloodthirsty, man-eating monsters, and reveals the reality of sharks as pillars in the evolution of the seas. Filmed in HD video, the movie exposes the exploitation and corruption surrounding the world's shark populations in the marine reserves of Cocos Island, Costa Rica and the Galapagos Islands, Ecuador. Rob teamed up with renegade conservationist Paul Watson, and their adventure starts with a battle between the *Sea Shepherd* and shark poachers in Guatemala, resulting in pirate boat rammings, gunboat chases, mafia espionage, corrupt court systems and attempted murder charges, forcing them to flee for their lives. Rob discovers these magnificent creatures have gone from predator to prey, and how they could easily be wiped out within a few years owing to human greed.

Positive results: since its release in 2007, *Sharkwater* has been seen by more than 124 million people, inspired the creation of several conservation groups including Fin Free (finfree.org), and has helped change Government policy worldwide. Today more than a hundred countries have banned shark-finning, and shark fin imports to China are estimated to have dropped 90%.

Other Achievements: winner of over forty international awards, *Sharkwater* continues to screen at festivals and events worldwide. *Sharkwater* broke box-office records in Canada as one of the biggest documentary releases in history, and has been published online with free viewing on YouTube as a tool for the shark conservation movement. Further information from **www.sharkwater.com**

And then there was *Revolution*. Rob Stewart's second documentary, *Revolution*, has received both critical and audience acclaim and has won many awards at film festivals around the world. The film is Rob's response to the pleas of leading scientists and conservationists, who told him that the bigger picture of the planet being in jeopardy needed to be told. They made the convincing case that by the middle of this century we could have no fish in the sea, no coral reefs, no rainforests and a planet failing to sustain many forms of life, including our own.

Revolution is an 82-minute documentary about opening your eyes, changing the world and fighting for something. Discovering that there's more in jeopardy than sharks, Rob uncovers a grave secret threatening our survival as a species, and embarks on a life-threatening adventure through four years and fifteen countries into the greatest battle ever waged. Featuring some of the most incredible wildlife spectacles ever recorded, *Revolution* brings audiences face to face with sharks and cuddly lemurs, into the microscopic world of the pygmy seahorse, and on the hunt with the deadly flamboyant cuttlefish. From the coral reefs in Papua New Guinea to the rainforests in Madagascar, Rob reveals that our fate is tied to even the smallest of creatures.

Through it all, Rob's journey reveals a massive opportunity, as activists and individuals all over the world are winning the battle to save the ecosystems we depend on for survival. Startling, beautiful, and provocative, *Revolution* inspires audiences across the globe to join the biggest movement in history that's rising to the challenge of saving our world. *Revolution* premiered at the Toronto International Film Festival in 2014.

As part of *Revolution's* unique distribution strategy, 50% of the proceeds from its release through the platform Yekra will benefit conservation groups such as Virgin's Ocean Unite, and Earth Justice. Groups and charities can host, play, stream and sell the movie to support their own initiatives. "The conservation movement is the biggest that has ever existed," says Rob Stewart. "It should be winning the battle to save our world ... all that's missing is awareness. We hope by releasing *Revolution* in this exciting way that we can help educate and empower everyone to get involved." The film will also be distributed to classrooms worldwide to educate and empower those whose future is at stake. Further information from **http://therevolutionmovie.com**

During the making of *Revolution*, Rob was contacted by an elementary school teacher in Saipan who had shown her young students his previous film, *Sharkwater*. The students were so inspired by the film that they got involved with their local government, resulting in Saipan banning shark fins. This triumph underscored to Rob what a difference a film can make, and that humanity will do the right thing once educated about an issue.

Ethics

Several companies have their own ethical rules for wildlife/conservation documentary-makers. The organisation Filmmakers for Conservation (FFC) has produced a set of principles and guidelines for working in the field as follows:

Filmmakers for Conservation: Principles

1. Always place the welfare of the subject to be filmed above all else

2. Ensure that your subjects are not caused any physical harm, anxiety, consequential predation or lessened reproductive success by your activities

3. Don't do anything that will permanently alter the natural behaviour of your subject. Be aware that habituation, baiting, and feeding may place your subjects at risk and may be lethal to them

4. It is unacceptable to restrict or restrain an animal by any means to attract a predator

5. Subjects should never be drugged or restrained in order to alter their behaviour for the sole purpose of filming

6. Be aware of and follow all local and national laws regarding wildlife where you are filming

7. Be courteous to your contributors (give appropriate credit where it is due). Whenever possible give copies of the finished programme, a copy of a long edit of an appropriate scene, and/or publicity photographs to the people who helped you

8. Images or scripts that give an audience abnormal, false or misleading information about a subject or its behaviour should be avoided

9. Always research your subject before filming.

Filmmakers for Conservation: General Guidelines for Working in the Field

- Restore all sites to their original state before you leave (for example, prepare scenes by tying back, rather than cutting, vegetation)

- Be aware and take precautions, as some species will permanently quit a site just because of your odour

- Keep film, video equipment, and crew-members at a distance sufficient to avoid site or subject disturbance

- Night shooting with artificial lights can require precautions to avoid making the subject vulnerable to predation

- Be prepared to meet unexpected conditions without damaging the environment or subject. Be especially prepared and deal with any people attracted by your activities, as they could put the subject at risk

- Be aware that filming a den or nest site could attract predators

- The use of tame or captive animals should be acknowledged in the film credits. If using tame or captive animals:

  a. Ensure the subject receives proper care
  b. The subject's trainer or custodian should always be present during filming.

In addition to the FFC principles and guidelines above, key ethical points to implement are:

1. **Provenance: captive versus wild**. The wildlife and conservation film-making community has a provenance decision to make on each production. The desire to film animal behaviour accurately will be paramount but the production budget, schedule or opportunity may not be sufficient to capture the behaviour by filming in the wild. It is unscrupulous to remove animals from the wild for entertainment purposes but it is acceptable to film animals where there is evidence that they are the third generation of the species to be kept in captivity.

2. **Welfare**. Film-makers have a responsibility to ensure that no animal is harmed in any way because of the film-making process; therefore, no filming

should take place if it puts the animal at risk of disturbance, physical damage, predation or if the filming would interfere with its breeding success.

a) The sourcing of animals should be carefully considered. The experience and credentials of the suppliers should be checked fully by an appropriate person (species expert, vet, animal welfare representative) reviewing evidence, provided by the supplier, that the conditions the animals are housed in are suitable for the well-being of the species involved.

b) Ideally, no animals would be moved purely for the purpose of filming; but if this is unavoidable they must be transported in secure, comfortable conditions and the journey should be as short as possible. Food and water must be provided and the animals be examined by an expert or vet on arrival.

c) Filming can be a stressful time for animals and very few production or camera crews are familiar with how to assess this. Experts in animal behaviour can advise film-makers on what is appropriate for the species being filmed. Researching the natural behaviour-patterns of a species will identify the conditions under which animal behaviour can be replicated for the camera. Equipment can inadvertently be harmful, lights can burn delicate eyes or burn fragile skin, and lenses can reflect an animal's appearance, thus suggesting to the animal that it has a rival, which could cause a change in its behaviour. Further, putting the animal in unfamiliar surroundings can stress it.

d) When an animal has been filmed it should be returned to its original location as soon as possible. However, this is possible only if so doing presents no threat to other animals in the area, eg if there is no risk of pathogens being introduced.

e) Misrepresentation of behaviour. Conservation film-makers should tell the truth about an animal's behaviour and not reinforce misconceptions in the public domain. For example, the destructive image of King Kong in the famous movie has contributed to a false belief that the gentle mountain gorilla is to be feared.

f) Film-makers should be aware of the impact their film may have on the desirability of animals to the audience. When an animal is revealed as cute, cuddly, funny etc it encourages the audience to obtain one for themselves, which can have a devastating impact on some species: eg female orangutan are killed, and their babies taken for the pet trade.

g) Some species are given special protection owing to their vulnerable status; film-makers are therefore required to abide by all welfare requirements if they have succeeded in gaining a licence to film these species.

h) Consider the habitat used in the filming location and take care not to cause any damage – it is home to a diversity of creatures. Visits to a site should be kept to a minimum to avoid damage to vegetation; the site should be restored to its natural state between visits.

i) A hide should not be erected if it attracts attention from the public. Moving hides towards a strategically-located site needs to be done step-by-step, with suitable intervals between moves.

j) Drones should be used with caution when flying over vulnerable species, especially at breeding time.

k) Hibernating animals should never be awakened for filming.

l) Threatened species such as otters, red squirrels and dormice are given full protection under Schedule 5 of the Wildlife and Countryside Act. The restrictions for filming these species at their place of shelter are the same as those for nesting birds.

m) Bats need special care as disturbance at, or near, a breeding colony of any bat may cause desertion of an otherwise safe site. All bats are specially protected and require a filming licence from the appropriate statutory body.

n) Some species are protected from trapping, including shrews, hedgehogs and pine martens. If these species are required for filming purposes a special licence will need to be obtained from the authorised awarding organisation.

o) For cold-bloodied animals and invertebrates, temporary removal from the wild to a studio or vivarium for filming is not recommended, but if this is unavoidable and a subject is removed from the wild it should be released as soon as possible into its original habitat.

p) Film-makers should be clear about legislation regarding wild plants. It is an offence to uproot wild plants without permission. For over a hundred threatened plants, including orchids, the law extends to picking the plants/flowers, so any damage to vegetation while filming should be avoided.

Further Reading

Wildlife Film-making: Looking to the Future edited by Piers Warren, foreword by Neil Nightingale – published by Wildeye 2011

What does the future of wildlife film-making hold for us all? Whether you are a budding film-maker, an experienced amateur or a seasoned professional, this new book – an accompaniment to the hugely successful *Careers in Wildlife Film-making* – attempts to answer this question. As technology advances rapidly and viewers' options increase, this book presents a unique collection of views and advice that make it an invaluable resource for everyone who wishes to succeed as a wildlife film-maker in years to come. With articles from many leading figures in the industry and case studies of numerous skilled practitioners.

(see www.wildeye.co.uk/shop.html)

Careers in Wildlife Film-making by Piers Warren – published by Wildeye 2002, 2006

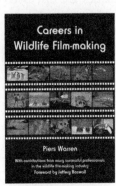

The essential book by Piers Warren, packed with guidance and advice for aspiring makers of natural history films. Described as 'long-overdue' and 'much-needed', this is not just an essential book for newcomers and wannabes - the fascinating case studies of well-known individuals, and unique discussion of the future of the industry from top professionals, make this an important read for those already working in the fields of wildlife, underwater and conservation film. Contents include: How Wildlife Films are Made, The variety of Jobs, How to Get Started, Education and Training, Wildlife Film Festivals, Organisations, Projects and Further Information, The Future of the Industry.

(see www.wildeye.co.uk/shop)

Confessions of a Wildlife Filmmaker: The Challenges of Staying Honest in an Industry Where Ratings Are King by Chris Palmer – published by Bluefield Publishing 2015

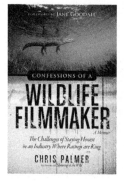

Chris Palmer's new book is part memoir, part confession, and part indictment of the cable and television networks for failing to put conservation, education, and animal welfare ahead of ratings and profits. It's also about the mistakes he's made while struggling to excel in a profession he loves. He argues that the state of the wildlife filmmaking industry worsens every year and says that it's time for wildlife filmmaking to move in a more ethical direction. He makes a compelling case that we must make broadcasters like Animal Planet, Discovery, National Geographic, and the History Channel do better, and that it's time for viewers and film-makers to fight back.

Shooting in the Wild: An Insider's Account of Making Movies in the Animal Kingdom by Chris Palmer – published by Sierra Club Books 2010

Longtime producer Chris Palmer provides an in-depth look at wild animals on film, covering the history of wildlife documentaries, safety issues, and the never-ending pressure to obtain the "money shot." Marlin Perkins, Jacques Cousteau, Steve Irwin, Timothy Treadwell, and many other familiar names are discussed along with their work, accidents, and in some cases, untimely deaths. Chris Palmer is highly critical of Irwin, and offers fascinating revelations about game farms used by exploitative film-makers and photographers looking for easy shots and willing to use caged animals to obtain them. He also considers the subliminal messages of many wildlife films, considering everything from *Shark Week* to *Happy Feet* and how they manipulate audiences toward preset conclusions about animal behavior. In all this is an engaging and exceedingly timely look at a form of entertainment the public has long taken for granted and which, as Chris Palmer points out, really needs a fresh and careful reconsideration.

Media, Ecology and Conservation: Using the media to protect the world's wildlife and ecosystems by John Blewitt – published by Green Books 2010

Media, Ecology and Conservation focuses on global connectivity and the role of new digital and traditional media in bringing people together to protect the world's endangered wildlife and conserve fragile and threatened habitats. By exploring the role of film, television, video, photography and the internet in animal conservation in the USA, India, Africa, Australia and the United Kingdom John Blewitt investigates the politics of media representation surrounding important controversies such as the trade in bushmeat, whaling and habitat destruction. The work and achievements of media/conservation activists are located within a cultural framework that simultaneously loves nature, reveres animals but too often ignores the uncomfortable realities of species extinction and animal cruelty.

Save the Humans by Rob Stewart – published by Random House Canada 2013

Beginning with a childhood spent catching poisonous snakes and chasing after alligators, Rob Stewart, the award-winning documentary film-maker behind *Sharkwater* and *Revolution*, charts his development into one of the world's leading environmental activists. Risking arrest and mafia reprisal in Costa Rica, nearly losing a leg in Panama and getting lost at sea in the remote Galapagos Islands, Stewart is living proof that the best way to create change in the world is to dive in over your head. With his efforts to save sharks leading to tangible policy change in countries around the world, Stewart sets his sights on a slightly bigger goal: saving humanity. Criss-crossing the globe to meet with the visionaries, entrepreneurs, scientists and children working to solve our environmental crises, Stewart's message is clear: the revolution to save humanity has started, the only thing missing is you!

187

Go Wild with your Camcorder - How to Make Wildlife Films by Piers Warren – published by Wildeye 2006

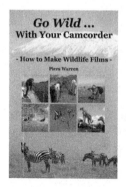

Whether you want to film wildlife as a fascinating hobby, or are hoping for a career as a professional wildlife film-maker, this book and a basic camcorder are all you need to get started! Packed with information and advice acquired over years of teaching wildlife film-making Piers Warren guides you through all aspects of making a wildlife film from choosing a camcorder to editing the final product. Also includes sections on: choosing subjects for filming, documentary themes, camera techniques, fieldcraft and set building.
(see www.wildeye.co.uk/shop)

Celebrity and the Environment by Dan Brockington – published by Zed Books 2009

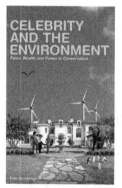

The battle to save the world is being joined by a powerful new group of warriors. Celebrities are lending their name to conservation causes, and conservation itself is growing its own stars to fight and speak for nature. In this timely and essential book, Dan Brockington argues that this alliance grows from the mutually supportive publicity celebrity and conservation causes provide for each other, and more fundamentally, that the flourishing of celebrity and charismatic conservation is part of an ever-closer intertwining of conservation and corporate capitalism. Celebrity promotions, the investments of rich executives, and the wealthy social networks of charismatic conservationists are producing more commodified and commercial conservation strategies; conservation becomes an ever more important means of generating profit. 'Celebrity and the Environment' provides vital critical analysis of this new phenomena and argues that, ironically, there may be a hidden cost to celebrity power to individual's relationships with the wild. The author argues that whilst wildlife television documentaries flourish, there is a significant decline in visits to national parks in many countries around the world and this is evidence that at a time when conservationists are calling for us to restore our relationships with the wild, many people are doing so simply by following the exploits of celebrity conservationists.

The Great Animal Orchestra: Finding the Origins of Music in the World's Wild Places by Bernie Krause – published by Profile Books 2012

A fascinating and unique exploration of nature's music, from plants and animals to wind and rain. Bernie Krause is the world's leading expert in natural sound. He has spent the last forty years recording ecological soundscapes and has archived the sounds of over 15,000 species, but half of the wild soundscapes he has on tape no longer exist because of human actions. Krause divides natural sound into three categories: biophony is the sound made by animals and plants, like the shrimp that makes noises underwater equivalent to 165 decibels; geophony is natural sound, like wind, water and rain, which led different tribes to have different musical scales; and anthrophony is human-generated sound, which affects animals as it changes, for example causing disoriented whales to become beached. In *The Great Animal Orchestra* he invites us to listen through his ears to all three as he showcases singing trees, contrasting coasts and the roar of the modern world. Just as streetlights engulf the stars, Krause argues that human noise is drowning out the sounds of nature.

Time-lapse Photography: A Complete Introduction to Shooting, Processing and Rendering Time-lapse Movies with a DSLR Camera by Ryan A Chylinski – published by Cedar Wings Creative 2012

An excellent guide to the techniques of creating time-lapse sequences with 350+ easy to understand examples, workflows, walkthroughs and diagrams covering basic and advanced topics. The book covers time-lapse gear from basic to advanced: tripods, intervalometers and remote timers, DSLR cameras and lenses; balancing time-lapse image settings; shooting time-lapse: composition and exposure; preventing time-lapse flicker; creating the time-lapse movie: codecs and frame rates, software workflows and walkthroughs; time-lapse challenges: astrophotography time-lapse, flicker-free day to night transitions, HDR time-lapses and time-lapse motion control devices. Throughout the book there are many links to online examples of time-lapse sequences. Author Ryan Chylinski is an American photographer and founder of LearnTimelapse.com, a community powered time-lapse education and experimentation hub.

About the Authors

Madelaine Westwood is the Founder of GAFI (Great Apes Film Initiative) and the Pedal-Powered Cinema Projects in Africa and SE Asia. She is also a former president of Filmmakers for Conservation. As a wildlife film-maker for over twenty years, Madelaine has learned that moving images can have a powerful effect on the people who view them: she has a background in documentaries – working with broadcasters such as National Geographic, BBC, Discovery, Channel 4 – plus five years in commercials and corporate films. Having produced films for conservation charities such as the RSPB, Madelaine decided to use this experience to try and reach the people who needed to see the films the most – those who live and work in the areas most affected by environmental damage, climate change, habitat loss and species extinction.

In order to create a template for how media could be used in conservation Madelaine concentrated on one endangered animal group to start with – Great Apes – founding the Great Apes Film Initiative in 2005. Initially this meant getting permission to screen films to local communities, decision-makers, armies, rangers, schools and local politicians – all those groups who contribute to changing their own environment. There have been constant challenges, but the results have been extraordinary. To date over 300 million people have seen wildlife and conservation films in fifteen of the states where great apes range – people who had never even seen a film have walked up to twenty miles to be in the audience. Many projects are flourishing: tree planting, bee-keeping, cane rat farming, organic farming, regular radio presentations; wildlife clubs are being set up, teachers are promoting sustainability, there's an active schools twinning programme between UK and Uganda. But there is always more to do.

Most of the areas GAFI works in do not have electricity, but the Pedal-Powered Cinema (where projectors are powered by bicycles) has solved the problem so

GAFI can screen conservation and local issue films in remote areas. The next step is to train people in local communities to make their own films, in their own languages, and help them to distribute their messages effectively. The media template for GAFI is now being used by partner NGOs to protect Asian elephants and tigers. The objective for Madelaine is to empower everyone committed to protecting and preserving our planet to create the change they want to see, by using one of the most powerful communication tools we have – the media.

madelaine@nutshellproductions.co.uk
www.nutshellproductions.co.uk
www.gafi4apes.org

 **Piers Warren** has been the Principal of Wildeye – the International School of Wildlife Film-making – since he founded it in 1999. He is also well-known throughout the wildlife film-making industry as the founder of *Wildlife Film News* and as the former producer of wildlife-film.com, which he created in the 1990s. With a strong background in biology, education and conservation, and a lifelong passion for wildlife films, Piers has a wide knowledge of natural history. He cut his teeth in the industry as a sound engineer and multi-media producer, running a studio for many years.

He is one of the founders of the international organisation Filmmakers for Conservation, and was its vice-president for the first three years. Piers is the author of many magazine features and numerous books including *Careers in Wildlife Film-making* and *Go Wild with Your Camcorder – How to Make Wildlife Films*.

piers@wildeye.co.uk
www.wildeye.co.uk

Wildlife-film.com has been the leading source of information for the wildlife film-making industry worldwide and Google's number one ranked site for 'wildlife film' and related searches for many years. The website is viewed in over 175 countries.

Our monthly newsletter, *Wildlife Film News*, is read by thousands of people involved in wildlife film-making – from broadcasters and producers to freelancers and newcomers – we encourage readers to submit their news.

Wildlife-film.com also serves as an online resource for industry professionals and services. Find producers, editors, presenters and more in the **Freelancer** section, and find out about festivals, training and conservation etc in **Organisations**. We encourage amateur and professional freelancers to join our network and welcome all wildlife-film related organisations to join our team.

We are committed to supporting **conservation film-making**. If you are a conservation organisation, or individual, we would love to have you come onboard as a member, so that we can promote your good work.

Apply for discounted or complimentary membership here:

www.wildlife-film.com/conservation

CPSIA information can be obtained
at www.ICGtesting.com
Printed in the USA
BVOW06s1400131116

467351BV00011B/8/P